THE PROBLEM OF
WAR
IN THE
OLD TESTAMENT

THE PROBLEM OF WAR IN THE OLD TESTAMENT

by PETER C. CRAIGIE

WILLIAM B. EERDMANS PUBLISHING COMPANY
GRAND RAPIDS, MICHIGAN

Library of Congress Cataloging in Publication Data

Craigie, Peter C.
    The problem of war in the Old Testament.

    Bibliography: p. 113.
    Includes index.
      1. War—Biblical teaching. 2. Bible. O.T.—
Criticism, interpretation, etc. I. Title.
BS1199.W2C72   261.8'73   78-17698
ISBN 0-8028-1742-4

Contents

Preface

This short study has been written for the Christian reader of the Old Testament. It is written with the conviction that its central problem, the problem of war, troubles many Christians. Because this is an important issue, one which has serious ramifications for contemporary Christian attitudes about war, this study has also been written with Christian educators in mind. In some places, the book becomes a bit technical; for those who hate footnotes, my advice is simply to ignore them.

Sometimes a piece of autobiography helps to explain the origin of a book; that is the case with this one. I began my adult life serving in the Royal Air Force, but later I turned to the study of theology. I expected a contrast in moving from the squadron to the college, but I found less of a contrast than I had anticipated. My research in the Old Testament took me to the study of early Hebrew poetry, and most of that poetry had associations with war. The difficulty of understanding the relationship between war and religion thus developed over a number of years. The problem was never merely intellectual or academic for me; rather, it was an issue intimately related to my practice of Christian living. It was from that issue, and from reflection on it, that this brief study emerged.

CHAPTER ONE

The Contemporary Problem of War in the Old Testament

milḥamah / מלחמה

(Genesis 14:2/Daniel 9:26)

I

The Hebrew word *milḥamah*, "war," occurs more than three hundred times in the Old Testament; it is to be found in the earliest as well as the latest writings. The frequent use of the word is disturbing in a book which is associated so intimately with the Prince of Peace. And *milḥamah* is only one of several Hebrew words associated with the various facets of warfare.

For the sensitive Christian reader of the Old Testament the frequent references to war create a variety of problems. These problems are essentially of two kinds. First, there are those personal, internal problems which arise from the attempt to grapple with the predominance of war in a book which is fundamental to the Christian faith. The books on war by Josephus, Herodotus, and other ancient historians do not create problems, for we have come to expect war to be a basic theme of history writing, both ancient and modern.[1] But war is a problem in the Old Testament exactly because it is *not* primarily a history book; rather, it is believed to be a part of God's revelation to mankind. Second, there are problems of an external nature; the presence of so much

---

1. Michael Grant, a distinguished classical scholar, has suggested that war is not only the most frequent, but also the most important subject matter of ancient history: see his *Ancient History* (New York: Harper Torchbook, 1965; first published in 1952), pp. 128–152.

martial material in the Old Testament has provided in the past, and continues to provide in the present, a basis from which a critique may be launched against the Christian Bible, or against the Christian faith. Let us examine in a little more detail each of these two types of difficulty.

II

The first group of problems was described as being of a personal nature for the Christian, though it relates also to the Christian church as a whole. These problems arise because the Old Testament continues to be read privately in personal devotion and publicly in services of divine worship; it has become a part of the inner life of Christianity.

It is disturbing—or at least it *should* be—for the Christian to read the ruthless laws of war in Deuteronomy 20:10–18, or to meditate upon the bloodthirsty execution of war in the books of Joshua and the Judges. In fact, however, there are different reactions to this warlike material; perhaps I can illustrate them from personal observations. I have known many Christians who have for a long time been devoted and daily readers of the Bible. For many of them war is no longer a problem, if it ever was, for as they read, a process of "spiritualization" takes place. For example, they can read of the capture of Jericho by the forces of Joshua and rejoice in the whole chapter, for translated into spiritual terms it describes the victory of those totally committed to God. I do not want to dispute such spiritual meaning, but I simply want to stress that read at face value the chapter describes the literal slaughter of men *and* women, young *and* old, all in the name of obedience to God (Joshua 6). A similar event in Vietnam was followed by a war crimes trial. Thus before the spiritual implications are drawn from such a text, some serious thought must be given to what it actually states.

There is another kind of reaction to the Old Testament, however, and it comes from those less accustomed to reading the Bible systematically. I belonged to a congregation a few years ago with no tradition of studying the Bible. We began a "Book of the Month" club, reading privately an Old Testament book one month and a New Testament book the next month; at the end of the month we met to discuss our discoveries and our problems. During the second month, we read I Kings and then met for discussion; the substance of that discussion was illuminating. Although we recognized that there were "good" parts, in general we reacted against the book, especially against the warlike material in it. Consequently, the group tended to have a somewhat negative attitude towards the Old Testament as a whole. For such people, clearly, some kind of solution must be found to the problem of war in the Old Testament, if ever that book is to become meaningful to them in public worship or private devotion.

What, then, are the dimensions of the problem of war in the Old Testament for the Christian? Though specific problems may vary from one reader to the next, there are three principal areas of difficulty.

First, there is the *problem of God,* or the theological problem. Stated succinctly, the problem lies in the fact that one of the dominant representations of God in the Old Testament is that of God as Warrior. It is not easy to reconcile this conception of God with the New Testament description of God as loving and self-giving.

Second, there is the *problem of revelation.* The problem here is complex; it is related in part to the manner of God's self-revelation in war, and in part to the preservation of war literature within the corpus of the written Word of God. Granted that wars took place in ancient Israel, as they do in the modern world, why was it necessary for so much of the literature of war to be preserved as a part of the revealed Scripture?

Third, there is the *problem of ethics.* Once again, the problem is complex. Are ethical teachings in Christianity to be based on the New Testament alone? Or may they be developed on the basis of the whole Bible? If all the Bible has relevance for ethics (the Ten Commandments, after all, are contained in the Old Testament), does it follow that war may be pursued legitimately? But if war may be pursued legitimately, would this position not appear to be somewhat in conflict with the New Testament?

From this brief summary of potential difficulties it is clear that a part of the overall problem is linked to the relationship between the Old Testament and the New Testament. Indeed, it will be necessary to turn to the New Testament in seeking solutions to these problems. But it is necessary to make certain provisions as to the way in which the New Testament is to be used. Before calling on the New Testament for help, we must make every effort to understand the Old Testament in its own right. And we must be very careful from the start not to lay aside too easily the Old Testament and its difficulties and to imply that it is, in effect, "second class" revelation in contrast to the New Testament. To be faithful to our Christian legacy, it is necessary to keep the whole Bible; alternatively, one may reject the whole Bible. It is very difficult, however, to settle in a half-way house, for the canonical Scriptures include both Testaments; while the relationship between those Testaments may be difficult to understand, nevertheless to question a part of the canon of Scripture is to question the whole. To oversimplify a very complex issue, the canon of Scripture places us in a "take it or leave it" situation; either alternative may be chosen in honesty, but the logic of a mid-way position is dangerous. And finally, we should not forget that for the first Christian generation, prior to the writing and canonization of the New Testament, the Old Testament was the *only* written Scripture which Christians possessed. If the Old Testament was Scripture for Jesus and the first Christians, let us not lay it aside too lightly, however proper our appreciation of the New Testament may be.[2]

2. Now that the basic problems have been stated, it might be argued by some that the problems are in fact artificial, or alternatively that the problems are a modern phenomenon. I have argued elsewhere that war probably was not a problem, either to men in Old Testament times, or to the writers or compilers of the Old Testament; see P. C. Craigie, "Yahweh is a Man of War," *Scottish Journal of Theology* 22 (1969), 183–188. And John Yoder has warned of the danger of imposing our modern conceptions on Jesus and his disciples in relation to their understanding of this Old Testament material; see J. H. Yoder, *The*

III

In addition to those problems of a personal and internal nature, there are also problems of an external nature. A critique may be launched against the Christian faith, either on the basis of the warlike content of the Old Testament, or on the basis of the association between Christianity and war throughout most of its history. These two alternatives are not far apart, for in most instances the relationship between Christianity and war has been the result of a particular interpretation of the Old Testament.[3] In identifying such a critique of the Bible or the Christian faith, it is important to make a distinction. The critique may reflect an attack on Christianity by its opponents, but equally it may reflect the very genuine difficulties of those anxious to determine the truth of Christian claims, but unable to reconcile some of the claims (love, peace) with some of the evidence (hate, war).

The critique may be explicit: it may be argued simply that the long association between Christianity and war, finding its roots in the Old Testament and demonstrated through many centuries, indicates clearly that the Christian message cannot honestly be said to be one of God's love for man. For example, while I was writing this chapter, I attended a debate at the University of Calgary, centered on the provocative question: "Has Christianity done anything for anybody at any time?" One of the debaters was Madalyn Murray O'Hair, a distinguished and outspoken representative of atheism in the United States. During the course of the debate, she described her reaction, while still a young girl, to reading through the Old Testament during the course of a weekend. She said that she was shocked by the content, the killing, the brutality, the war, and so on. I have no doubt that this reaction was an honest one, and one that too few

---

Politics of Jesus (Grand Rapids: Eerdmans Publishing Co., 1972), pp. 86–89. Nevertheless, I would argue that the problem of war in the Old Testament, though in part a reflection of modernity, is real to modern Old Testament readers. But insofar as a proper understanding of the issues may be reached, they may cease to be "problems."

3. This topic is examined in more detail in Chapter 2.

Christian readers have, for the simple reason that familiarity with the text has, as it were, anaesthetized them to what it is actually saying. For Madalyn Murray O'Hair this reaction to the Bible contributed not only to her atheism but also to her forceful critique of Christianity.

Alternatively, however, the critique may be launched in a more veiled manner. For example, the influential seventeenth century philosopher, Spinoza, pointed to the negative implications of warfare for religion in the preface to a book, the *Tractatus Theologico-Politicus* (1670), containing a very influential attack on the Bible as revelation. The Bible, when Spinoza was done with it, had lost its authority and contained little more than a minimal deposit of relevance to ethics and piety.[4]

It may be valuable to bring home the force of this critique by referring to a recent, important study; the study presents the results of research and demands some careful self-examination on the part of Christians. The work in question is a monograph by Elbert W. Russell, entitled *Christianity and Militarism*.[5] Russell undertakes a study of attitudes towards militarism within Christianity. According to his conclusions, the more orthodox a Christian group or individual may be, the more likely it is that his attitudes will be militaristic. (The exceptions to this general rule are provided by "unorthodox" groups, such as Unitarians and Quakers; Russell is a Quaker.) Russell stresses the paradoxical nature of these results, because one of the professed aims of Christianity throughout its history has been *peace*. One further point from Russell's study should be noted: among several sources of militarism in Christianity, the Old Testament is identified as a principal source.

Two general comments may be made concerning Russell's

---

4. For a fuller account, see P. C. Craigie, "The Influence of Spinoza in the Higher Criticism of the Old Testament," *Evangelical Quarterly* 50/1 (1978), 23–32.

5. Published under the auspices of the Canadian Peace Research Institute; *Peace Research Reviews* 4/3 (1971). See further Frank Epp, *A Strategy for Peace: Reflections of a Christian Pacifist* (Grand Rapids: Eerdmans Publishing Co., 1973), p. 107.

position. First, the monograph is not expressly written as an attack upon orthodox or mainstream Christianity; in fact, the editor of the series adds a postscript in which he urges members of the Christian churches to undertake self-examination in relation to the issues which are raised. Second, while it might be possible to debate the validity of Russell's conclusions on the basis of certain limitations inherent in his method (the psychological study of attitudes), nevertheless the general validity of the conclusions seems self-evident, not only from the evidence of the history of the Christian church, but even from the role played (or, sometimes, not played) by major Christian bodies in relation to the events occurring in East Asia during the last three decades. The Christian churches, it is sad to say, do not have an unbroken tradition of univocal opposition to the evils of war; relatively speaking, the opposition to war has been proclaimed by lonely voices. And in this, Christianity is not unique, for all the world's major religious traditions, even those built on pacifist foundations such as Buddhism, have a record that is marred in places.[6] However, to summarize the purpose in introducing Russell's monograph, it is true that Christians must undertake some self-assessment in relation to the matter of war, not only for themselves, but also in order to deal with critiques from without. The criticism laid against the Bible or the Christian faith will elicit no clear response from Christians unless first they grapple with the problems and seek to understand them.

IV

Having stated the problems associated with war in the Old Testament, let us now try to clarify the reasons for studying the subject in detail. Five reasons will be suggested; some will summarize what has been said already, and some will introduce further important aspects of the subject matter.

6. For a detailed study of the relationship between war and the major religious traditions, see Guenter Lewy, *Religion and Revolution* (New York: Oxford University Press, 1974).

1. If we are to profit as Christians from reading the Old Testament, we must have an overall perspective with which to interpret its many passages dealing with war.

2. If we are to give an intelligent response to the criticism of the Bible or the Christian faith, we must first understand the problems for ourselves.

3. The third point opens up an even more vital reason for attempting to come to grips with the problem of war in the Old Testament. The third reason is rooted in the observation of a contemporary writer on war and peace. Anatol Rapoport, in an important essay on the philosophy of war,[7] has pointed to a distinction between *natural* phenomena (such as earthquakes, floods, drought) and *man-made* phenomena. Unlike natural phenomena, man-made phenomena are influenced to a very large extent by what the majority of human beings think and say about them. To be more specific, the future of war, a man-made phenomenon, will be determined largely by what men think and say about it. The attitudes and actions of Christian persons, though only one small section of human society, will have an influence on the future of war. But that influence may be either positive or negative. If Christians are to have clear attitudes towards war, they must first come to some understanding of the subject in the Bible, including the Old Testament.

4. The fourth reason for studying the problem of war in the Old Testament is intimately related to the third. The Old Testament, along with the New, is used extensively in Christian education, particularly in the education of the young. When the Old Testament is presented in this context as the Word of God, it will inevitably exert considerable influence in the formation of young people's attitudes. And yet at this point, there has been a curious tradition in Christianity; while human sexuality (something essentially good) has been treated with the greatest of caution, if at all, human conflict (something essentially evil) has aroused little anxiety. The point can be illustrated by one of the "Fathers" of

---

7. The essay is written as an introduction to a new edition of Carl von Clausewitz, *On War* (Harmondsworth: Penguin Books, 1968; the original German work was published in 1832). This work is discussed in more detail in Chapter 4.

the Christian church, who, though writing some sixteen centuries ago, represents both ancient and modern attitudes. Jerome, in a letter to the wife of a friend concerning her daughter, had this to say: "She should not read the Song of Songs [Song of Solomon] until she has read Chronicles and Kings, for otherwise she might not observe that the book refers only to spiritual love."[8] The point to be made concerns not Jerome's "Victorian" embarrassment with the beautiful love poetry of the Song of Solomon, but rather the fact that he saw no difficulties in a young girl ploughing through the warlike material in Chronicles and Kings! A different perspective is provided by an educational writer from the earlier half of the current century, Marion J. Benedict: "For educators to use these writings [the war passages in the Old Testament] without historical background and independent ethical judgment, and hence to teach children that God instigates and uses warfare is, to say the least, not likely to develop aversion to war."[9] Benedict's own interpretation of war in the Old Testament is now somewhat dated, but the point she makes is an important one. Her concern is with the *attitudes* that children develop towards war, and so she attempts to suggest a curriculum of such a kind that the Bible might be influential in the formation of peaceful rather than warlike attitudes. This is an important point; before we can deal with this topic in the education of children, however, we must seek first to understand the Biblical text ourselves.

5. The final reason for studying the problem of war in the Old Testament relates to the fundamental character of the century in which we live. All the centuries of human history have been characterized by an admixture of war and peace, but in the twentieth century there have been global wars in addition to regional wars, wars on so great a scale as to give a hollow ring to the grand talk of peace. But the two world wars of this century have been overshadowed by an even more significant event. On August 6, 1945, the first atomic weapon to be used in war was dropped on

8. The passage is cited in H. J. Schonfield, *The Song of Songs* (New York: Mentor Books, 1959), p. 12.

9. Marion J. Benedict, *The God of the Old Testament in Relation to War* (New York: Teachers College, Columbia University, 1927), p. 164.

Hiroshima; three days later a second bomb was dropped on Nagasaki. Those three summer days heralded the opening of a new era in human history, the age of human omnipotence.[10] Developments in nuclear research and the stockpiling of nuclear weapons have provided mankind with a form of omnipotence; unlike the creative omnipotence of God, that of man is destructive only, for it lies in his ability to destroy all living things in less than six days. In order to live with the threat of this terrible power, most men have developed a moral insensitivity to it,[11] but thereby they have increased the danger. In such a century as this, Christians must ignore neither the potential threat of nuclear disaster nor the multitude of "minor" wars, for we are all citizens of this globe and its future rests, in part at least, in our hands. A responsibility is placed upon us to try to understand the dimensions of modern warfare, conventional and nuclear,[12] and then to seek the avenue in which we might work for peace. I am not sure that conscientious objection to war will provide a full solution, but nevertheless some words of the late President John Kennedy indicate the radical nature of the change that will be required of us: "War will exist until that distant day when the conscientious objector enjoys the same reputation and prestige that the warrior does today."[13] But again, if we are to form a clear understanding of the nature of war and peace and of our role in relation to them, we must first seek to clarify the Biblical basis of our position.

V

In the light of these introductory comments, the approach to be taken in the following chapters will be clarified. First, a brief

10. See further P. C. Craigie, "Hiroshima After Thirty Years: Reflections on the Politics of Omnipotence," *The Chelsea Journal* 1/4 (1975), 163–166.

11. See R. W. Gardiner, *The Cool Arm of Destruction: Modern Weapons and Moral Insensitivity* (Philadelphia: Westminster Press, 1974).

12. For a useful introductory guide to the subject, see Alastair Buchan, *War in Modern Society: An Introduction* (London: Collins, 1966).

13. The words are quoted in a letter from Representative (the Rev.) Robert F. Drinan, to *Time*, September 30, 1974, p. 17.

examination of the Old Testament's "legacy of war" will afford us a fuller understanding of the serious nature of the problem and of the necessity to study it. Then the principal areas of difficulty relating to war in the Old Testament will be taken up one by one, beginning with the problem of "God the Warrior." At this stage of investigation some aspects of the problem may become more, rather than less, acute, for to clarify a problem is not necessarily to solve it. Eventually, however, the elements of a provisional solution to the problem of war in the Old Testament will emerge: these will be brought together into a more unified perspective in the concluding chapter.

CHAPTER TWO

The Old Testament's Legacy of War

I

We saw in Chapter 1 some of the dimensions of the problem of war in the Old Testament for the Christian in the twentieth century. Now let us turn back in history to that period of time between the closing of the Old Testament (ca. second century B.C.) and our modern era. Throughout these two millennia, the Old Testament has continued to be read among Christians and Jews, and, in a different way, it has played a role in the religion of Islam. In each of these religious communities the Old Testament has had a greater influence than other types of writings. The reason is to be found in the nature of the book: it was not considered to be simply an historical book, but for Christians and Jews it was divine revelation, and for Muslims too it belonged to a special category. As revelation, the Old Testament affected men's beliefs and actions, for its revelatory status carried with it divine authority. Not least of the matters on which the Old Testament exerted its influence was war. Men have used the Old Testament in the formulation of theories of war and the state, and in the practice of war; sometimes the theory and practice developed independently, and then the Old Testament was employed in an effort to justify and legitimate that theory and practice. But sometimes the influence of the Old Testament in relation to war has been more subtle and hence harder to trace.

Thus the Old Testament's legacy to subsequent generations has often been one of war; that is, its influence in matters of religious faith and practice has promoted in certain ways the use of war by men and nations. The influence may be quite illegiti-

21

mate and may be based upon a fundamental misinterpretation of the meaning and purpose of the Old Testament, but the fact that the Old Testament has indeed left us this legacy invites an examination of it. The examination will serve, among other things, to remind us of the dangers implicit in the misreading of the Old Testament, and, more importantly, it will bring home to us the urgency of continued study of the problem of war in the Old Testament for ourselves and our own age, lest inadvertently we too repeat the errors of the past.

The paragraphs which follow do not contain a systematic analysis of the Old Testament's influence on matters of war over two millennia. Rather, three short portraits are provided, drawn respectively from the history of Islam, Christianity, and Judaism, to illustrate how profound and effective the Old Testament's influence has been. The limits of the study have been deliberately extended at this point beyond the confines of Christianity and the Christian interpretation of the Old Testament. Too often, relations between Christians, Muslims, and Jews have been marred by conflict, and that conflict has been based on similar ideology, rooted in some sense in the Old Testament. A broader perspective at this point may contribute broader understanding among Christians of the nature of the other religious traditions.

II

A key aspect of the Islamic religious tradition is designated by the word *jihād,* but the term has often been misunderstood, both within Islam and, more frequently, in the Western world. Literally, *jihād* means "struggling" or "striving," though it is often rendered as meaning "holy war." The early Islamic lawyers distinguished between four kinds of *jihād*/striving: (a) *jihād* of the "heart" (spiritual striving); (b) *jihād* of the "hand" (physical striving, work, labor); (c) *jihād* of the tongue (striving in preaching or debate); (d) *jihād* of the "sword" (striving in war, hence "holy war," since the striving, of all kinds, was to be "in the way of

Allah/God").[1] Thus, technically, *jihād* implies war only in a limited sense, and even in that context, most modern Muslim interpreters argue that the word was used exclusively in the sense of *defensive* warfare.[2] However, warfare was employed in the earliest history of Islam, beginning in the time of the prophet Muhammad. And the Old Testament was influential to some extent in the formulation of the religious ideology of war in Islam.[3] Let us then examine the use of war in the time of Muhammad, first in general terms, and second with specific reference to the Old Testament.[4]

Muhammad was born in Mecca about 570 A.D. From about the year 610 he felt a growing conviction that God (Allah) was calling him to a prophetic ministry and giving to him revelations, the essence of which was a profound religious and social message to his fellow Meccans (Arabs living in Muhammad's home-town, Mecca). For almost ten years (ca. 613–622 A.D.), the prophet preached his message to his fellow citizens, and, though he gained followers, he also aroused strong opposition from the established merchants of Mecca. The opposition eventually became so severe that in the year 622 the Emigration *(Hijrah)* from Mecca took place, and Muhammad and his fellow Muslims set up their new headquarters in the oasis at Medina, more than 200 miles to the north of Mecca. The Emigration,

1. For a detailed analysis of this subject, see M. Khadduri, *War and Peace in the Law of Islam* (Baltimore: Johns Hopkins Press, 1955).

2. In addition, modern interpreters of the *Qur'an* attempt to mitigate as far as possible the militaristic aspects of *jihād*; see J. M. S. Baljon, *Modern Muslim Koran Interpretation* (Leiden: Brill, 1968), pp. 108–109. For an interpretation of *jihād* as essentially defensive warfare, see Hammudah Abdel-Ati, *Al-Jihad in Islam* (Islamic Culture Administration: Al-Azhar University, n.d.); Ahmad A. Galwash, *The Religion of Islam*, Vol. II (Studies in Islam Series, no. 13: Supreme Council for Islamic Affairs, Cairo, 1966), pp. 271–293.

3. The role of the Old Testament will be examined after a brief survey of the emergence of war in Islam.

4. The details of Muhammad's life and ministry are the subject of considerable academic debate. The positive interpretation given in the following paragraphs follows essentially the work of W. Montgomery Watt, *Muhammad, Prophet and Statesman* (London: Oxford University Press, 1961).

however, did not bring to an end the opposition to the prophet Muhammad from the Meccan merchants.

During the years in Medina the Muslims gradually began to assume the use of force in a religious context. Initially this can be seen in the use of the *razzia* ("raid"), a traditional and very limited form of conflict in Arabia. Conflict also emerged in a thoroughly defensive context, namely in the warding off of continuing Meccan aggression. Gradually, however, there was a transition from *defensive* war to *aggressive* war; war, still on a very limited scale, was utilized to achieve certain ends. Theoretically, even the aggressive warfare can be interpreted defensively; though aggressive in a purely military context, Muhammad's use of war was defensive in that it was the result, in the larger perspective, of prior Meccan aggression.[5]

The transition from defensive war to aggressive war (in the military sense) was probably marked by the Battle of Badr (624 A.D.), a desert battle between a small Muslim force and a superior Meccan army. In spite of the Meccan advantage in numbers, the Muslims were victorious and interpreted their victory as a vindication of their trust in God. The words "Prophet, urge the believers to fight" *(Qur'an* 8:65) probably reflect the elation of victory after Badr and the anticipation of further victories.[6] The historical evidence for the period after the Battle of Badr indicates a military policy that was more than simply defensive.

The interpretation of the victory at Badr in the *Qur'an* is presented in a highly significant context. As has been noted, *Qur'an* 8:65 appears to reflect the Muslim elation after Badr; in the same *surah* (chapter) there is a reference to the Old Testament account of God's victory over "the people of pharaoh" (8:55 ff.) in

5. The majority of the charges to fight contained in the *Qur'an* are set in a context indicating either self-defense or the prior aggression of the enemy; see, for example, *Qur'an* 2:190–193; 22:39–40. The principal difficulty, for those who wish to maintain that *all* fighting was defensive, is the so-called "Verse of the Sword" (9:6). N.B. references to the *Qur'an* in the text and notes follow the Egyptian Arabic edition.

6. Cf. W. Montgomery Watt, *Companion to the Qur'an* (London: George Allen and Unwin, 1967), pp. 95–99.

the Hebrew Exodus from Egypt. The Muslim ideology of war, as it is reflected in this portion of the *Qur'an,* is in fact very similar to the ancient Israelite ideology of war. When the Muslims engaged with unbelievers in battle (*Qur'an* 8:17), it was properly God, rather than the Muslims, who did the fighting; similarly, the Old Testament victory song celebrating the Israelite success over pharaoh and his army grants that victory to God, not to the Israelite warriors (Exodus 15:1–18). Allah, during the fighting, is the "Protector" of the Muslims (*Qur'an* 8:40), just as God is the "protection and refuge" of the Israelites (Exodus 15:2).[7] The use of language in this *surah* of the *Qur'an,* together with the explicit reference to the Israelite Exodus from Egypt, indicate quite clearly that there was a close parallel in Muhammad's thought between the Biblical Exodus (which marked the beginning of the Holy War tradition) and the Muslim experience in the Battle of Badr, and afterwards.[8] Whether Muhammad was familiar with the text of the Old Testament, or whether he knew its contents from Christian or Jewish acquaintances (there were Jews living in Medina), cannot be known with certainty. But it is clear that in

7. On the Exodus as the beginning of the "Holy War" tradition in Israel (which makes the parallel more striking), see the discussion in Chapter 4, below ("Holy War"). On the translation "protection and refuge" (Exodus 15:2), see P. C. Craigie, *Vetus Testamentum* 22 (1972), 146–147.

8. Further substantiation of the argument, though of a more technical nature, can be seen in the matter of *al-furqān*. The use of *furqān* in the *Qur'an* seems to have a double nuance; in places it has the standard meaning, "separation, division" (from the verb *faraqa*), but sometimes it means "salvation, deliverance," a sense presumably derived from (Christian) Syriac *pūrqānā*. In *Qur'an* 2:48–53, Moses receives "the book and *al-furqān*"; here the word refers to the "salvation, deliverance" of the Exodus, when "we [God] *divided* (*faraqna*) for you the sea." The parallel to this account of the Exodus is to be found in *Qur'an* 8:29, 41, in which the victory at Badr was interpreted as the "day of deliverance" (*yawn al-furqān*). The language further demonstrates the close relationship in Muhammad's thought between the Exodus and the Battle of Badr. For further discussion and sources, see E. W. Lane, *An Arabic-English Lexicon,* Bk. I, Part vi (New York: Frederick Ungar Publishing Co., n.d.), p. 2385; R. Bell, *Introduction to the Qur'an* (Edinburgh: Edinburgh University Press, 1953), pp. 136–138; *idem, The Origin of Islam in its Christian Environment* (London: Frank Cass & Co., 1968).

the matter of war, as in other matters,[9] Muhammad was influenced by the Old Testament in some fashion.

In the history of Islam, particularly in the dramatic expansion of its earliest centuries, there was a tendency for the militaristic aspects of the faith (viz., "jihād of the sword") to become of paramount importance. And in the modern Islamic world the militaristic aspects of the faith have occasionally reappeared, as in the heterodox Khaksar movement in India, to give a rather extreme example.[10] To some extent, this militant trait of the Islamic tradition finds its roots in the Old Testament. But to close on a more positive note, modern Muslim thought reflects for the most part a strong antagonism to war and is attempting to interpret the jihād-tradition in a most positive way.[11]

III

Within Christianity the Old Testament has exerted a more direct influence than in the case of Islam. The reason for the difference is to be found in the status afforded to the Old Testament within Christianity; it has been a part of the divine revelation and therefore an *authoritative* book. Consequently, Christian thinkers throughout the centuries have had to take the Old Testament into consideration when constructing political theories, particularly with reference to the matter of war. Whatever the political theory, it had to be squared with the Old Testament, and very often Old Testament support would be adduced for it. Within

9. For a detailed collection and discussion of Biblical materials in the *Qur'an*, see H. Speyer, *Die Biblischen Erzählungen im Qoran* (Hildesheim: Georg Olms Verlag, 1971; originally published in 1931).

10. The founder of the movement, "Al-Mashriqi," is said to have had discussions with Hitler on the subject of *jihād*. See further Baljon, *Koran Interpretation*, pp. 11-12; W. C. Smith, *Islam in Modern India* (Lahore, 1946).

11. See, for example, Munir Husain, "The Jihād of our Times," *Islamic Literature* (Lahore) 14/2 (1968), 19-22. See also the paper of K. G. Saiyadain, read to the International Inter-Religious Symposium on Peace (New Delhi, 1968), reprinted in H. A. Jack, ed., *World Religions and World Peace* (Boston: Beacon Press, 1968), pp. 49-57.

the Christian world the principle was so important that even political theorists who were not avowedly Christian had to give serious attention to the Old Testament in arguing their case, as did Thomas Hobbes in his *Leviathan* and Spinoza in his *Tractatus Theologico-Politicus.*[12]

Thus once again the Old Testament exerted an influence, though it was of doubtful legitimacy for the political theorists found little difficulty in adapting the teaching of the Old Testament in support of their teaching on war; in this, as in other matters, the history of Old Testament interpretation demonstrates an extraordinary relativity. Let us examine, by way of example, Exodus 32:26–28; the passage describes the slaughter of idol-worshipping Israelites by the Levites, following the direct commandment of God.[13] For Augustine the passage described an act of persecution directed by Moses, who was seen as a secular magistrate; it provided for Augustine's own age a justification for the limited persecution of heretics by the secular magistrate. Thomas Aquinas, reacting perhaps to the spirit of the Crusades in his own time, interpreted the passage as a direct act of God without significance for the future and therefore not justifying the war of good men against evil men. John Calvin interpreted the passage as an example of the saints voluntarily executing the will of God; it provided a precedent for the saints of his own time, namely the "elect," to participate enthusiastically in war against evildoers.

The Old Testament's influence and legacy was to be seen also in spheres other than Biblical interpretation in the context of political theory (though note that the theories in the preceding paragraph were closely related to practice). Perhaps the most terrible of all the examples of the Old Testament's influence is to

12. Thus Spinoza has the theoretical task of setting forth the nature of that state within which the philosopher would have freedom to philosophize, and yet almost the whole of his *Tractatus Theologico-Politicus* (1670) is focused on a critique of the Bible, especially the Old Testament.

13. The summary statements which follow are based on the careful study of Michael Walzer, "Exodus 32 and the Theory of Holy War: the History of a Citation," *Harvard Theological Review* 61 (1968), 3–14.

be seen in the Crusades; let us look briefly at the First Crusade by way of example. The first Crusade culminated in the capture of Jerusalem and the defeat of its Muslim defenders on July 15, 1099. It was a victory achieved by terrible bloodshed and slaughter. According to the Christian chroniclers of the event, some 10,000 Muslims were beheaded in the great Mosque, and on July 16 the vicinity of the Sacred Precinct was choked with blood and corpses. The chroniclers (mainly Christian clerics) recount these facts with joy and applaud the "justice" that was done.[14] The Crusade, launched, ironically enough, in an attempt to secure peace within Christendom, was a resurrection of the Old Testament's ideology of the Holy War. A favorite text of the Crusaders was drawn from the Old Testament: "Cursed be he that keepeth back his hand from blood" (Jeremiah 48:10).[15] The Crusades, of course, must be interpreted in the light of a variety of complex forces within and beyond medieval Christendom; the Old Testament did not launch the Crusades, but it was made to provide a theoretical base for them, and the perpetrators of that terrible crime on July 15 apparently felt clear in their conscience when they claimed that their victory was the "justification of all Christianity."

These are but a few examples, to which others could be added; in the American Civil War, for example, both sides drew freely upon the Old Testament in the attempt to justify their cause.[16] But enough has been said to illustrate the potential influence of the Old Testament within Christianity towards the use of war. The lessons of our history evoke the serious attempt to study the Old Testament, to understand its message in the con-

---

14. John Gray, *A History of Jerusalem* (London: Robert Hale, 1969), pp. 236–237.

15. R. H. Bainton, *Christian Attitudes toward War and Peace* (Nashville: Abingdon Press, 1960), p. 112.

16. See further G. H. Gilbert, *The Bible and Universal Peace* (New York: Funk and Wagnalls, 1914). Perhaps the most powerful critique of this tradition is Mark Twain's "The War Prayer," reprinted in Kay Boyle and Justine van Gundy, *Enough of Dying: Voices for Peace* (New York: Dell Publishing Co., 1972), pp. 92–95.

text of the whole Bible, and to beware of the danger of manipulating its teachings to human ends.

IV

The Old Testament, or *Tanakh,* to give it its Jewish title,[17] has remained the central sacred text of Judaism; during the course of more than two thousand years of Jewish history, it has played, along with the Mishnah and Talmud, a formative role in the faith and practice of Judaism. The circumstances of the Jewish people have been such, however, that they have not, for the most part, been influenced by the Old Testament in the way that Christians have in relation to war. War is an act of the state (or perhaps, in a more limited sense, a combined act of rebellion against the state), and whereas there have been many so-called Christian states during the last two millennia, the Jews, both in Palestine and in the Diaspora, have been small communities within states. Far from being in a position to wage war, they have been the victims of prejudice and persecution. And, too often, Christians have been the ones responsible for that persecution of the Jews, forgetting that Jesus was a Jew and that he called his followers to love all men.

Only in the twentieth century, with the emergence of Zionism within Judaism, has an independent state of Israel emerged again for the first time since 586 B.C. Modern Israel is not technically a Jewish state in terms of its constitution; it is a secular democracy, though clearly it is a Jewish state in a more general sense. And Zionism is not in a specific sense a religious phenomenon, but is a form of secular messianism occurring

17. *Tanakh* is the Jewish title for the collection of books which Christians designate the "Old Testament." It is a composite word, made up of the first letters of the Hebrew titles for the three major sections of the Old Testament: *Torah* (Pentateuch), *Nebi'im* (Prophets), and *Kethubim* (Writings). For practical purposes, I will continue to use Old Testament in the following paragraphs, provided it is understood that this is Christian terminology for what, in context, is Jewish Scripture.

among the Jewish people.[18] Both Zionism as a movement and Israel as a state have been influenced by the Old Testament in a variety of ways. The central significance of the *land* and the concept of *return* are fundamental to Zionism. And even the most secular and socialist of Zionist leaders have drawn upon the Old Testament in expressing their ideas. David Ben Gurion, for example, a socialist and Zionist, and later Prime Minister of the new state of Israel, freely drew upon Biblical ideas and texts (Jeremiah 42–43) in writing *The Imperatives of the Jewish Revolution* (1944).[19]

One cannot compare this modern influence of the Old Testament in Zionism, however, with its influence in the history of Christianity. For Christianity the terrible influence exerted by the Old Testament from time to time was based on its character as divine revelation and thereby its appearance of providing divine authority and justification for the use of war. For the secular Zionists, however, the role of the Old Testament in shaping political ideology has a different character; it is a part of the ancient Jewish historical and cultural tradition and it is still a living tradition among the Jews. Its influence has been channeled primarily through the identification of the contemporary Jew with his ancestors and their land, but for most Zionists it has not been forced into the role of providing divine support for their worldly struggle.

Before leaving Judaism, let us turn back to an earlier period in Jewish history, partly in order to demonstrate further the influence of the Old Testament in matters of war, but partly also to introduce a more positive note for the conclusion of this depressing topic.

In the first century A.D., during the lifetime of Jesus, a political party emerged among the Jews of Palestine. The party, founded by Judas the Galilean about 6 A.D., decided upon a

18. There were—and are—many deeply religious Jewish Zionists, as well as many Zionists who are Jews, but not Judaists (men of faith). But in practical terms, Zionism can be seen as a thoroughly pragmatic and political movement.
19. For the text, see A. Hertzberg, ed., *The Zionist Idea* (New York: Harper Torchbooks edition, 1966), pp. 606–619.

solution to the problem of Jewish subservience to their Roman overlords; the party came to be referred to as the Zealots. While the Sadducees accepted the *status quo* of Roman rule, and served and ruled under the Romans, while the Pharisees were apolitical and sought to stress obedience to the divine law, and while the Essenes dropped out of mainstream life to await the time of the end, the Zealots advocated a more active policy. Violence and war alone could lead to the liberation of the Jewish people. Their ideology of war, having antecedents in the time of the Maccabees, can be traced back ultimately to the Old Testament. Israel had once been an independent state with its own king; it would be again, if the Zealots had their way.

After several decades of violent tactics, the climax came in the years 66–70 A.D. A Zealot uprising led to their capture of the fortress at Masada on the western side of the Dead Sea in 66, and soon afterwards the Zealots had also taken the city of Jerusalem. But they were participating in a lost cause against the massive resources of Rome, and, after a few years of struggle, the Roman armies of Titus recaptured Jerusalem in 70; by way of reprisal, the Jerusalem Temple was destroyed. Some Zealots continued their opposition from the fortress at Masada until the spring of 73 when at last they too were killed by Roman soldiers.

For Judaism as a religion defeat in war was not the really tragic element in this sad affair; a large number of the Jews had never wanted to fight against Rome in the first place. The tragedy was the destruction of the Temple in Jerusalem (it was not rebuilt), for that marked the end of an era in Jewish history. It is in the reaction of the Jews to that tragic destruction that a lesson is to be found, not only for Jews but also for contemporary Christians.

Jacob Neusner, a distinguished Jewish scholar, has drawn a stark contrast between the two options which faced the Jews following the destruction of their temple in Jerusalem; he describes those options as two roads leading out from Jerusalem.[20]

---

20. See Jacob Neusner, *A Life of Yohanan ben Zakkai* (Leiden: Brill, 1969), pp. 174–176.

One road led to the fortress at Masada; it was the road chosen by the Zealots, and at its end they fought bravely but futilely until all were killed by the Romans. To the end, they stood by their ideology of war and their vision of a return to Old Testament times. But if the future of Judaism had rested in the hands of the Zealots alone, the religion would have ended in the year 73.[21]

The other road led west from Jerusalem to Yavneh (Jamnia); this was the road chosen by some of the Jews, led by Yohanan ben Zakkai. In Yavneh was discovered the source of strength which Judaism required, following the demise of the Temple and its worship; that strength was found in the study of Torah and in the application of its teaching to every sphere of living.

V

Too often in the past Christians have taken the "road to Masada"; they have found in the Old Testament support and encouragement in their militaristic enterprises, but they have not seen the whole message which that book presents. The contemporary Christian, aware of the dangers of the past, must take the "road to Yavneh"—the road that leads to careful study of the Old Testament text and the translation of its principles into life and faith. The chapters which follow are not a substitute for walking along that road; they provide only guidance which might be helpful along the way.

> *My son*
> *Don't forget my* torah!
> *And may your heart preserve my commandments.*
> *For length of days,*
> *And long life,*
> *And peace* (shālôm)
> *Shall they add to you.*
>
> (Proverbs 3:1–2)

21. In fact, militant nationalism continued to exist in Judaism for a little more than 60 years after the destruction of the Zealot stronghold at Masada. It finally came to an end in 135 A.D. with the Roman suppression of the Bar Kochba Rebellion.

CHAPTER THREE

God the Warrior

Who is the King of Glory?
The Lord, strong and mighty,
The Lord, mighty in battle.

(Psalm 24:8)

I

The quotation from Psalm 24 provides a further example, in miniature, of the Old Testament's potential "legacy of war"; two persons from recent history will illustrate the point.

Before the Allied Forces landed in Normandy during the Second World War, General (later Field Marshall) Montgomery sent a message to his troops, the 21st Army Group. The message closed with these words: "Let us pray that the Lord Mighty in Battle will go forth with our armies, and that his special providence will aid us in the struggle."[1] Both the words and the desire reflect the Old Testament psalm, and the similarity is not a coincidence. Montgomery was a soldier who affirmed a simple Christian faith and who diligently read both the Old and the New Testaments. He believed that in response to prayer God would be with him and his men as they advanced into battle.

A second illustration is provided by General George S. Patton; on January 1, 1944, he wrote his famous "Soldier's Prayer": "God of our fathers, who by land and sea has ever led us to

1. A copy of Montgomery's message was shown to me by my former colleague, Professor Robert Osborne, Carleton University. For brief comments on Montgomery's religious faith, see particularly Ronald Lewin, *Montgomery as Military Commander* (New York: Stein and Day, 1971), pp. 21–22.

victory, please continue your inspiring guidance in this the greatest of our conflicts. . . . Grant us the victory, Lord."[2] Patton, like Montgomery, affirmed the Christian faith; he too read the Old Testament and believed in the efficacy of prayer in battle.

These two distinguished soldiers were not unique in associating God with war. Though they were not theologians in any formal sense, both read the Bible as Christian laymen and what they found in the Old Testament did not appear to conflict with their professional careers. In the past God the Warrior had fought on behalf of his chosen people, as the Old Testament clearly affirms. Then why should God not continue to be known as a Warrior in the modern world?

There has been a very different reaction to the conception of God the Warrior, however, from that represented by Montgomery and Patton. A Christian theologian, C. E. Raven, came to a very different conclusion in a work published just before the outbreak of World War II.[3] "Until lately, the Old Testament stood alongside the New as inspired. . . . Large parts of the Old Testament glorify the God of Battles rather than the Father of our Lord Jesus Christ." Raven could not reconcile the different portraits of God given in the Old and New Testaments. Because the God described in the Old Testament appeared to be so basically incompatible with the "Father of Our Lord Jesus Christ," the implication was that the Old Testament must go.[4]

---

2. The "Soldier's Prayer" is quoted from H. Essame, *Patton: a Study in Command* (New York: Charles Scribner's Sons, 1974), p. 253.

3. C. E. Raven, *War and the Christian* (London: S.C.M., 1938), p. 51.

4. The tradition of rejecting the Old Testament, largely on the basis of the warlike character of God, has a long history in Christianity, going back at least as far as Marcion in the second century A.D. Marcion developed a kind of dualism between the "weak" and cruel Creator God of the Old Testament and the loving, merciful God of the New Testament. Eventually he became a heretic and developed a form of Gnosticism. Marcion fixed a canon of scripture for his movement, including certain Pauline Epistles and the Gospel of Luke, but in this action he showed the larger issues involved in his position; in order to maintain a consistent position, he was forced to excise certain Old Testament allusions from the Gospel. The implication for the contemporary Christian is clear; to reject the Old Testament will result in a shrunken form of the New Testament. It should be added that although C. E. Raven was an unorthodox theologian, he was in no sense a Marcionite.

These contrasting illustrations have been employed deliberately to bring into focus the dilemma which faces the contemporary Christian reader of the Old Testament. God is clearly associated there with the wars of ancient Israel. And yet, just as clearly, the New Testament leads us to believe that war and the God of Christian faith should be totally antithetical. Are we not enjoined to love one another, even our enemies (Luke 6:27)? And is not this because God himself is love? Can God be both loving and warlike? The immediate answer would seem to be: No! And yet simply to reject the Old Testament altogether is too radical, for it has been a part of the Christian Bible from the earliest of Christian generations.

II

A solution to the problem is required which will enable us to understand the meaning of the conception of God the Warrior, without simply rejecting it out of hand, or, alternatively, rejecting the Old Testament itself. To find such a solution, it will be necessary to examine the Old Testament and attempt to understand something of the context in which God is described as a Warrior. Only then may it be possible to determine whether this conception is primitive or "pre-Christian," whether it is essentially alien to the Christian faith, or whether there is in fact something profound to be learned from the conception of God the Warrior.

First, however, it must be stressed that the theme of God the Warrior is an important one in the Old Testament, not something peripheral to the main subject matter. The words from Psalm 24, quoted at the beginning of this chapter, are in no sense unusual in their implication, for there are many other places in the Old Testament where God is associated directly with warfare. Similar words are found in the "Song of the Sea" (Exodus 15:1–18), in which the introductory verses of praise extol the Lord as a "Man in Battle."[5] But perhaps even greater significance is to be

---

5. Or: "the Lord is a *Warrior*" (*gibbôr*), following the Samaritan text.

found in one of the titles which the Old Testament writers used regularly of God: "Lord of *Hosts*" (literally *Armies*). The title is used more than two hundred times in the Old Testament and although its precise significance is not clear in every context, the earliest meaning of the title clearly associates God with the armies of Israel.[6] Furthermore, the frequent association of the title "Lord of Hosts/Armies" with the Ark of the Covenant is significant (e.g., II Samuel 6:2), for the Ark symbolized God's presence on the battlefield alongside his people (see particularly Numbers 10:35–36).

Such examples can be multiplied.[7] The people of Israel were commanded to fight and kill their enemies by the law of God (Deuteronomy 20:10–18). It was God who destroyed the Egyptian army in the sea (Exodus 15:21) and God who brought victory to his friends and disaster to his enemies (Judges 5:31). Before the army departed for war, God was consulted (Judges 1:1; 20:18); when victory had been won, the spoils of war were dedicated to the Lord, in theory at least (I Samuel 15). There are many similar texts which contribute to the implications of the concept of God the Warrior, but what is the meaning of all this data for the modern reader? Is there a solution to the problem created by this warlike material? Before suggesting a solution, it is necessary to cut off a "line of retreat" from the problem which is taken by many Christian readers of the Old Testament without realizing the theological implications of the retreat.

III

The line of retreat from the problem may be expressed in a variety of ways. For example, the conception of God as Warrior may be

6. For further discussion of the title, see particularly P. D. Miller, *The Divine Warrior in Early Israel* (Cambridge: Harvard University Press, 1973), pp. 145–155; W. Eichrodt, *Theology of the Old Testament*, Vol. I, trans. J. A. Baker (London: S.C.M., 1961), pp. 192–194.

7. Marion Benedict concluded: "In fact, the book of Ruth is practically the only entire document [in the Old Testament] in which Yahweh is not

said to be a primitive, pre-Christian notion; the Hebrews were simply identifying their God with war in the same way that other nations did at that time. They were, after all, an unsophisticated people (unlike ourselves!) with a coarse and lowly view of God, which was eventually to be outgrown in New Testament times. Implicit in this superficial line of argument is an important assumption, namely that the conception of God as Warrior is simply a human interpretation of God, and not revelation of God's nature and activity. Since it is merely human interpretation, so it is argued, the conception of God as Warrior can be dispensed with and replaced with a loftier, less primitive conception of God as Love.

From a theological perspective, however, there is a subtle danger in this line of argument. It involves the mistake, first of all, of confusing a view of progressive revelation (with) a developmental (or evolutionary) theory of religion.[8] By progressive revelation is meant the view that God's self-revelation may increase and that therefore more may be known of him over the passage of time, but the progression in revelation does not contradict or cancel out the earlier substance of revelation; it can only complement that substance. But the implication of the summary argument which has been given is that the Old Testament contains not God's self-revelation, or a record of that revelation, but that it portrays man's search after God.[9] Theologically, in other words, the argument amounts to a rejection of the Old Testament *as revelation;* the Old Testament does not contain the divine self-

common
✱ mistake

---

directly or indirectly associated with warfare" (*The God of the Old Testament in Relation to War,* p. 163). Two other exceptions are the Song of Solomon and Esther, for God is not mentioned by name in either of these texts (though Esther has its share of warlike material).

8. It should be stressed that the view against which I am arguing could be legitimately sustained strictly within the context of the discipline of the *history of religion,* but (in my judgment) it cannot be sustained theologically. The argument which follows is theological, not historical, in nature.

9. On the predominance of this premise in much of modern Biblical scholarship, see T. W. Manson, "The Failure of Liberalism to Interpret the Bible as the Word of God," in C. W. Dugmore, ed., *The Interpretation of the Bible* (London: S.C.M., 1944), particularly pp. 101–102.

disclosure, but rather, in the context of war, it contains mankind's primitive attempts to interpret essentially human events as demonstrating the activity of God. God, the Hebrews thought, was a Warrior, but now that mankind has come of age, the primitive notion can be rejected.[10]

There are further difficulties with this line of retreat from the problem. One of them is that it results in the omission of one of the most significant and central aspects of Old Testament theology;[11] this point should become clearer as the chapter progresses. But in addition, the line of retreat also introduces problems for the understanding of the New Testament. Neither Stephen nor Paul rejected the conception of God as Warrior, as is evident from their references to God's great deliverance of Israel from Egypt, the event which marked the inauguration of the conception of God as Warrior in ancient Israel (see Acts 7:35–36; 13:17). Hence, an attempt must be made to seek a more positive interpretation of the Old Testament's description of God as Warrior.

IV

The words "the Lord is a Man in Battle" (Exodus 15:3) are employed in an ancient hymn in which the Israelites celebrated their Exodus from Egypt. After the Israelites had passed safely through the sea, their Egyptian pursuers were drowned. Al-

10. I am deliberately being gently cynical, for the view against which I am reacting contains (probably unconsciously) much of the arrogance of the nineteenth and twentieth centuries. Too easily, it may be assumed that the extraordinary developments in science and technology are paralleled by developments in ethics and morality. But in the matter of war, mankind has not clearly progressed, and may indeed have regressed from the standards of the Biblical period.

11. On the importance of the theme for Old Testament theology, see particularly the following works: G. E. Wright, *The Old Testament and Theology* (New York: Harper and Row, 1969), pp. 121–150; P. D. Miller, "God the Warrior: A Problem in Biblical Interpretation and Apologetics," *Interpretation* 19 (1965), 39–46; R. Tomes, "Exodus 14: the Mighty Acts of God: An Essay in Theological Criticism," *Scottish Journal of Theology* 22 (1969), 455–478.

though in a strict sense the events associated with the Exodus cannot be described as a military engagement, for the Israelites did not actually fight, the Exodus was nevertheless celebrated as a mighty victory in war. The Lord had defeated the elite forces of the Egyptian pharaoh, who was believed in ancient Egypt to be the divine son of the Great God. The Lord was a Warrior, the Hebrews believed, who was more powerful in battle than the greatest world power of that time!

The victory of God over Egypt in the Exodus has particular importance for the understanding of religion in the Old Testament, for it illustrates one of the two principal modes of divine revelation. These modes are respectively: (a) God's self-revelation through the *spoken word* (e.g., the words of God spoken through Moses or the prophets); (b) God's self-revelation by means of *participation in human history*. It is the latter form of revelation which is illustrated in the Israelite Exodus from Egypt; God is said to have participated directly in that event and he revealed thereby his presence and his power to his chosen people.

The Hebrew conviction that God revealed himself in the events of human history provides a clue to understanding the conception of God as Warrior. The primary affirmation concerning God in the Old Testament is that although he is transcendent,[12] the living experience of the immanent God is to be found within the fabric of human history. The experience of God in human existence can only be expressed in human terms, for otherwise God (ultimately transcendent) could not be known at all. As a learned rabbi put it in the Talmud: "We describe God by terms borrowed from his creation, in order to make him intelligible to the human ear."[13]

To call God a Warrior is to use anthropomorphic language, the language of immanence.[14] Like all human language it is

---

12. The transcendence of God is affirmed primarily in the various creation narratives (e.g., Genesis 1:1-2).

13. Cited in I. Epstein, *Judaism: A Historical Presentation* (Harmondsworth: Penguin Books, 1959), p. 137.

14. See further P. C. Craigie, "Hebrew Thought about God and Nature and its Contemporary Significance," *Canadian Journal of Theology* (1970), pp. 3-11.

limited and from a theological perspective it points to a truth about God which is greater than the language itself. Thus the conception of God as Warrior contains a theological insight, but it points to a truth greater than the words which convey ¡:. We must look further at the words expressing that truth if we are to understand it.

A further examination of Israel's past indicates that God's self-revelation in the Exodus was not typical of all his participation in Israelite history, for the Exodus is described essentially as a miraculous event. In the account of the military conquest of the promised land which followed the Exodus, a different aspect of God's participation may be seen. During the conquest the Israelites fought in real wars against real enemies, but still it was God who granted to them the victory in battle. In circumstances such as these the self-revelation of God was not to be seen primarily in miraculous events, but simply in his working through the human activities of his chosen people. God determined, in some sense, the outcome of human events by participating through the *normal* forms of human activity; God, as Warrior, fought *through* the fighting of his people. Let us consider further the implications of the divine activity being channeled through normal human activity.

God's self-revelation through participation in human history is sometimes described by the expression "Salvation History" (*Heilsgeschichte*).[15] The expression is helpful, first because it serves as a reminder that the Hebrew understanding of history is radically different from modern conceptions, and second, because the words "Salvation History" indicate that God's participation in history has a particular end in view. History, in the Biblical

15. See, for example, the earlier writings of G. E. Wright, (*God Who Acts: Biblical Theology as Recital,* 1952) and G. von Rad (*Old Testament Theology,* Vol. I, 1960; Vol. II, 1962) for perspectives on *Heilsgeschichte.* This approach to the nature of the Old Testament has often been pursued too exclusively, or too much has been claimed for it in studying ancient Israel in its Near Eastern context; see J. Barr, *Old and New in Interpretation* (London: S.C.M., 1966), pp. 65–102; Bertil Albrektson, *History and the Gods* (Lund: Gleerup, 1967). In the present context, the expression "Salvation History" is being employed in a broad and general sense.

writings, is not an enclosed system, a sequence of causes and effects, nor even something determined solely by human will and action.[16] Though human will and action are fundamental, history moves and develops, in some sense, within the providence of God. Again, history is not limited to past events; rather, the participation of God which can be perceived in past events, is involved also in the present moment of history, and it points towards a culmination lying still in the future. That point of culmination is salvation.[17] From the perspective of the Christian reader of the Old Testament, the immediate culmination of that history—the immediate salvation—is to be found in the coming of Jesus, though that event was not the final culmination.

Given this perspective on the nature of "salvation history," it becomes clear that the human beings through whom God acts in history are not perfect or sinless, for the primary object of God's participation is man's salvation. Since God participates in human history precisely to achieve this end, it is evident that the people through whom he acts, and the world in which he acts, are in need of salvation and are therefore imperfect.

This broad perspective can now be focused on the particular issue of warfare. War is a human activity; furthermore, it is a sinful human activity, revealing man's inhumanity to his fellow man. To describe God as a warrior is thus to say that God participates in human history, through *sinful human beings,* and through what have become the "normal" forms of human activity. Insofar as God is active in the world through human lives, he is employing for his purpose sinful persons. To state it another way, God employs, for his purpose of bringing salvation to the world, the very human beings who need salvation.

One point is becoming very clear: the activity of God in this world, insofar as it involves human beings as agents, must always appear, to a greater or lesser extent, to be associated with sinful-

16. Cf. G. Hasel, *Old Testament Theology: Basic Issues in the Current Debate* (Grand Rapids: Eerdmans Publishing Co., 1972), pp. 81–95.

17. It is significant to note that "salvation" in the Old Testament is a translation of a Hebrew word which has the primary sense of "victory, deliverance" (in war).

ness. But there is another side to this difficult statement. The participation of God in human history and through human lives does not primarily afford us a glimpse of his moral *being;* it demonstrates rather his will and *activity.* [18] God acts to bring man salvation, and in this activity he does not limit himself to the *miraculous,* [19] but participates in all aspects of human existence.

The argument so far, however, has by no means completely resolved the problem of God the warrior; at best, it has provided a larger context for understanding the problem. The conception of God as Warrior does not legitimize warfare, nor does it mean that a noble end has somehow justified war as a means to that end. Theoretically, it may be said that God, the giver of all life, has the absolute and only authority to withdraw life, or to command war in which it will be withdrawn. It may also be said that the wars of Israel could only be "justified" by divine command, for such a right pertains only to God. But any such statement must be prefaced by the understanding that the divine activity takes as its stage the *world as it is,* [20] namely the world of sinful men and activities, and this understanding is the primary condition for understanding war: *war is always evil.* The participation of God through evil human activity has a positive end in view; that is to say, the judgment of God, in the larger perspective, is the other face of the coin which is the mercy of God. Hence, on some occasions the reasons for God's exercise of sovereignty in war may be made evident (e.g., the punishment of evil men and nations by Israel, or the punishment of Israel by foreign nations), but they may remain as much a mystery as the initial mystery of God's creation of, and gift of, life.

The difficulty with which this chapter began has been only

18. See further W. Eichrodt, *Theology of the Old Testament,* Vol. I, pp. 228–229.

19. Insofar as divine activity is *miraculous,* it frees us from the moral dilemma of God the Warrior. God's withdrawing of the lives of the Egyptian army in the sea is no more problematic than his withdrawing the life of the aged Moses. He exercises the right to withdraw lives which he gave in the first place.

20. See P. C. Craigie, *Scottish Journal of Theology* 20 (1969), 186; G. E. Wright, *The Old Testament and Theology,* pp. 129–130.

partially reduced; it will have to be re-examined from different perspectives in subsequent chapters. But already certain preliminary perspectives are beginning to emerge which are relevant to the problem. The first point is this: war appears to be an ever present reality of historical existence, both ancient and modern. If God is King, the ultimate sovereign of human history, it is to be expected that he will stand in some kind of relationship to war. We perceive, though not always clearly, that war is a form of evil human activity in which God participates actively for the purposes of both redemption and judgment; in this participation, God is the Warrior.

The second point is that the conception of God as Warrior provides *hope* for sinful mankind. If the precondition for experiencing the presence of God in human, historical existence were that the persons and activities concerned must be sinless, then it is clear (from a Biblical perspective at least) that God's presence in history would never be known at all. God as Warrior is a conception which proclaims to mankind, in the most forceful language, that even in his human dilemma, with the concomitant human sin, he may seek for God and find him.[21] God's presence in such a situation (war, for example) will not justify it or make it holy, but it does provide hope in a situation of hopelessness.

21. A similar dilemma, and a similar resolution, may be seen (in the context of Hinduism) with reference to the *Bhagavad Gita,* whose teaching is presented in the context of war. See further K. N. Upadhyaya, "The Bhagavad Gita on War and Peace," *Philosophy East and West* 19 (1969), 159–169.

CHAPTER FOUR

The Problem of "Holy" War

You shall devour all the nations which the Lord
your God is about to give over to you. Spare none of
them, and do not worship their Gods. . . .

(Deuteronomy 7:16)

I

The harsh words of the opening quotation are startling in the context of Holy Scripture. They are presented in the Book of Deuteronomy as part of an address delivered by Moses to the Hebrew people, assembled on the plains of Moab. Moses, speaking on behalf of God, was preparing his people for the conquest and conflict which lay in their immediate future. The words introduce for us the other half of the problem of the previous chapter. Not only was God identified as a Warrior, but he commanded his chosen people to engage in a war of aggression; it is this aggressive or "holy" war which must now be examined.

The exhortation to war contained in Deuteronomy 7 is supplemented by laws of war contained in Deuteronomy 20, which again are presented as part of the address of Moses. In Deuteronomy 20:10–18, a two-fold military policy of conquest is presented. First, when the Hebrews approached cities lying outside their promised land, they were to offer the terms of a peace treaty; if the offer was rejected, they were to besiege the city and slay all its males, but women and children could be spared and taken as the spoils of war. The second part of the policy, however, applied to cities lying within the territory of the promised land. Such cities were to be besieged, and after they had fallen, all living creatures within the cities were to be put to death.

45

It is instructive to compare these ancient laws of war with the theory of Carl von Clausewitz, a Prussian soldier and philosopher of war (1780–1831). Von Clausewitz defined war as "an act of violence intended to compel our opponent to fulfil our will."[1] As a part of his analysis of war he made an important and necessary distinction between the theoretical or abstract conception of war, on the one hand, and real wars on the other hand. From the theoretical perspective, war must end in victory for the aggressor, for otherwise it would be pointless to initiate war in the first place. If complete victory was to be obtained, then no effort could be spared; for von Clausewitz, "to introduce into the philosophy of war itself a principle of moderation would be an absurdity."[2] The reality of war differed from the abstract conception of it only in that certain factors might arise, such as chance or the psychological state of the enemy (morale), which could not have been foreseen theoretically.

Von Clausewitz argued that from a military perspective there were three principal objects in warfare. First, the military power of the enemy must be destroyed, so that the enemy could no longer undertake war. Second, the enemy's country must be conquered, for from that country a new military force could emerge. Third, war could only be terminated finally when the enemy's will to fight had been subdued.

Let us now examine the laws of war in Deuteronomy in the light of the theory of von Clausewitz. It is clear, first of all, that the legislation in Deuteronomy 20 concerns wars of conquest;[3] the wars were to be acts of violence by which the Hebrews compelled their opponents to fulfill their (and God's) will. It is also clear that the laws for dealing with enemies do not introduce a principle of moderation, but are thoroughly pragmatic in a military sense. Although the treatment of cities outside the promised land was to be less harsh than that assigned to cities within the land, nevertheless that distinction was simply a part of the overall

---

1. C. von Clausewitz, *On War* (Harmondsworth: Penguin Books, 1968), p. 101. Initially published in 1832 under the title *Vom Kriege*.
    2. *Ibid.*, p. 102.
    3. The text of Deuteronomy 20 is examined in more detail in my *The Book of Deuteronomy* (NICOT, Grand Rapids: Eerdmans Publishing Co., 1976).

policy. Cities outside the promised land would eventually become neighbors of the new state of Israel; they would receive a warning concerning Israel's military capacity, but they were not the prime military target. The legislation concerning cities within the promised land, however, was of a terminal nature and without moderation. In this section of the law (20:16–18), all three of von Clausewitz's military objectives would be achieved in a single stroke. The military power of the Hebrews' predecessors in the land would be destroyed, the country (or city state) would be conquered so that no new army could emerge, and the will of the enemy would have been mortally subdued.

Deuteronomy 20:10–18, however, contains the laws of war, which are essentially theoretical in their construction; as von Clausewitz observed, there could be a difference between the theory of war and the reality and practice or war. In the actual Hebrew experience of war the laws were by no means fulfilled in every instance. The military commander Saul, for example, was condemned on one occasion for being insufficiently thorough in his execution of the laws of war (I Samuel 15). But more often than not, the laws of war seem to have been executed with considerable ruthlessness, as becomes evident from reading the Book of Joshua. (The historicity of these events has been questioned and will be discussed later in the chapter.)

To summarize what has been said so far, war in ancient Israel was a harsh reality. If the reality of war may not always have matched the legislation and theory concerning war, nevertheless the fact of aggressive warfare remains implanted in the earlier Old Testament books. The manner in which both the theory and practice of war are presented in Scripture is such that it is clear that the wars of the Hebrews were *religious* wars; that is, they were initiated and carried out within the context of religion. And to quote Baron de Jomini, a French philosopher of war and contemporary of von Clausewitz, "religious wars are above all the most deplorable."[4] After reading Deuteronomy 7 and 20, together

---

4. Baron de Jomini, *The Art of War* (reprinted by Greenwood Press: Westport, Conn., n.d.), p. 31. The first English translation was published in 1832.

with the war narratives of Joshua, Judges and Samuel, it is hard
to find disagreement with de Jomini. But to say that the wars of
conquest described in the Old Testament were *religious* wars is not
necessarily the same as saying that they were *holy* wars. The word
holy implies something which is intrinsically good and pure in
itself. Can war, even war in the context of Biblical religion,
properly be called holy? Let us examine this conception in a little
more detail.

II

The expression "holy war" is not derived from the Biblical texts.
This observation, however, does not remove the difficulty, for the
Biblical expression is equally forceful; the Biblical writers referred
to the "Wars of the Lord" (see Numbers 21:14; I Samuel 18:17;
25:28; etc.). The wars that were undertaken in ancient Israel had
a specifically religious character to them. Before the tribes of
Israel went to war, they consulted God for guidance. The warriors
who marched into battle had to be consecrated to God, putting to
one side anything impure. As they entered the arena of battle,
God's presence with them was symbolized by the ark of the
covenant. When victory had been won, songs were sung in praise
of the victorious God in a victory celebration.

This religious dimension of warfare must be understood in
the context of the covenant faith of early Israel. From the time of
Abraham, the Hebrews had anticipated the fulfillment of God's
promise of a land. That ancient promise was renewed in the
covenant made at Sinai, but between Sinai and the plains of
Moab it became clear that the realization of that ancient promise
would be by means of warfare. Through fighting the Canaanites
and thereby executing upon them the judgment of God, the
Israelite tribes would take possession of their inheritance which
God had promised of old.

But still the problem remains. While it is clear that the wars
were *religious* in character, were they *holy*? Did God's command
and God's presence transform something essentially evil into a

holy act? Can the ruthless requirement for the extermination of the enemy—men, women, and children—in any way be regarded as holy? I think that it can not!

In fact, the validity of the expression "holy war" is questionable, but it represents one important dimension of contemporary Old Testament scholarship on the matter of war. Although the expression has been used for some time by Biblical scholars,[5] it has found its most articulate expression in the studies of a distinguished German scholar, Gerhard von Rad.[6] Von Rad argued that war in ancient Israel was a cultic act undertaken by the amphictyony (the cultic confederation of Hebrew tribes); it was holy precisely because it was a *cultic* act, not simply an act that had religious dimensions to it.[7] But von Rad's view, in many of its details, has been criticized and modified by a number of scholars, and gradually a consensus seems to be emerging that the wars of ancient Israel should not be called "holy war," but "Yahweh war."[8] While war was religious by association, it was no more a cultic and holy act than was sheep shearing.[9]

Thus, it would perhaps be wise to drop the expression "holy war," the origins of which appear to be Greek,[10] and to refer

5. One of the earliest uses of the expression was by Fr. Schwally, *Der heilige Krieg im alten Israel* (Leipzig, 1901).

6. *Der heilige Krieg im alten Israel* (Göttingen: Vandenhoeck und Ruprecht, 1965. First published in 1951). *Idem, Studies in Deuteronomy* (London: S.C.M., 1953), pp. 45–59.

7. Note, however, that in von Rad's reconstruction, very few *real* wars took place in early Israel. The war narratives are a construction of *Heilsgeschichte* but were not rooted in any historical reality. The few wars that did take place in the time of the Judges are all described by von Rad as *defensive* wars, though it should be noted that such an hypothesis is in evident contradiction of the intention of the writers of the earlier Old Testament books.

8. R. Smend, *Yahweh War and Tribal Confederation,* trans. M. G. Rogers (Nashville: Abingdon Press, 1970). M. Weippert, "'Heiliger Krieg' in Israel und Assyrien. Kritische Anmerkungen zu Gerhard von Rads Konzept des 'Heiligen Krieges im alten Israel,'" *ZAW* 84 (1972), 460–493. F. Stolz, *Jahwes und Israels Kriege. Kriegstheorien und Kriegserfahrungen* (ATANT, 60, Zurich: Theologischer Verlag, 1972). G. H. Jones, "'Holy War' or 'Yahweh War'?" *VT* 25 (1975), 642–658.

9. G. Fohrer, *Geschichte der israelitischen Religion* (Berlin: de Gruyter, 1969), p. 109.

10. See G. H. Jones, *VT* 25 (1975), p. 642.

either to "Yahweh war" or to the "wars of the Lord." But the distinction between "holy war" and "wars of the Lord," though important in the academic debate, does not remove the problem which is central to this chapter. The fact remains that aggressive wars were carried out (or are reported to have been carried out) at the command of God, in the name of God, and with the help of God. And even if it is argued that the Biblical "historical" narratives have a legendary character to them, and that the wars of conquest described therein did not actually take place,[11] still the problem remains. For although the historical reality of the wars of conquest may perhaps be removed in this manner, the theological ideal remains. That is, if in fact there were no real wars of conquest, it seems clear enough on the surface that the Old Testament writers intended to convey to us the impression (albeit ideal) that there were, and in the last resort it is the written word, rather than the historically vague event lying behind the word, which constitutes Holy Scripture.[12]

III

Let us approach the problem of the aggressive theory and practice of war in ancient Israel from a modern perspective. In the modern world, war can have a subtle effect on those who do not experience its reality at first hand. War is a terrible business, but out of its darkness certain positive human qualities may emerge, such

11. For M. Noth, for example, there was no conquest in the conventional sense, but rather a generally peaceful settlement of tribes in Palestine; *The History of Israel*, 2nd ed. (London: A. & C. Black, 1960).

12. This view is held in opposition to that of G. E. Mendenhall, *The Tenth Generation: The Origins of the Biblical Tradition* (Baltimore: Johns Hopkins University Press, 1973). For Mendenhall, the origin of the Biblical community is to be found in a kind of revolution, involving the acceptance of the dominion of Yahweh and the rejection of force. But whatever the historical merits of this thesis, and however great its appeal may be in the modern world, it is nevertheless a very different picture from that conveyed by the Biblical writers, and it rests, in the last resort, not primarily on the text of Scripture, but on an historical and socio-anthropological analysis of the earliest history of the Biblical community.

things as courage, faith, and hope. Very often it is these positive by-products of war, and not war itself, which are brought home to those who view war from a distance. These positive by-products may be extolled by the novelists and film makers, and perhaps this is not wrong, for even in disaster mankind will look for some ray of redeeming hope.

But for the truer picture of war one must turn to the soldier or the inhabitants of a land in which war has been waged. The reality of war is to be found in fear, death, and destruction, in the bodies of soldiers shattered by shrapnel, in bombed houses collapsing on their inhabitants, in starving orphans desolate in streets, and in the rape, looting, and sadistic cruelty which are the negative by-products of war. Wilfrid Owen, a poet of the First World War, has captured something of the horror of a gas-attack in these lines:[13]

Gas! Gas! Quick, boys!—An ecstasy of fumbling,
Fitting the clumsy helmets just in time,
But someone still was yelling out and stumbling
And floundering like a man in fire or lime.
Dim through the misty panes and thick green light,
As under a green sea, I saw him drowning.

In all my dreams before my helpless sight
He plunges at me, guttering, choking, drowning.

If in some smothered dreams, you too could pace
Behind the wagon that we flung him in,
And watch the white eyes writhing in his face,
His hanging face, like a devil's sick of sin;
If you could hear, at every jolt, the blood
Come gargling from the froth-corrupted lungs,
Bitter as the cud
Of vile, incurable sores on innocent tongues,—
My friend, you would not tell with such high zest,
To children ardent for some desperate glory,
The old Lie: Dulce et decorum est
Pro patria mori.

13. From "Dulce et Decorum Est" in E. Blunden, ed., *The Poems of Wilfrid Owen* (London: Chatto and Windus, 1921).

The old Lie—"sweet and proper it is to die for one's country"—has for centuries veiled the terrible reality of warfare, just as terrible now in the 1970s as it was in the First World War.

But for Christians the tendency to underestimate the horror of war, which arises from viewing it at a distance, may be further compounded by an ancient Christian doctrine (though it is not so ancient as the New Testament). That doctrine is the theory of the "Just War," the roots of which are to be found in the writings of Ambrose and Augustine in the fourth and fifth centuries A.D., and which is still maintained by most major Christian denominations in the twentieth century. The popular title is not quite fair to the doctrine, for it does not advocate so much that certain wars may be "just," but rather that certain wars may be "justified." There is, however, an important aspect of this doctrine which may contribute to the common Christian underestimation of the horrors of war. According to the "Just War" theory, there were certain rules of conduct which were to be observed in war; there was to be no unnecessary violence, no needless destruction, no looting, no large-scale massacre of populations, and no acts of vengeance or reprisal. The spirit of such legislation may seem admirable and it foreshadows such later agreements as the Geneva Convention. And yet, in spite of the positive qualities, there is an unrealistic character to this advocacy of just conduct in war. It is clearly the product of religious persons, rather than military philosophers.[14] Such legislation would have been ridiculous for von Clausewitz. Such noble and "just" behavior in warfare could only be advocated if it contributed directly to achieving victory; as a principle of moderation it would be harmful, for it could seriously undermine the whole purpose of going to war in the first place.

14. Augustine's views on war are contained in various writings, but his most important work in the larger context is his *City of God*. Written in the aftermath of war, namely the capture of Rome by Alaric, the book has a certain realism to it in spite of the critical comments made here. My point is not that Augustine had no understanding of the reality of war, for that does emerge in the *City of God,* but that he did not have the ruthless pragmatism of a military commander.

The foregoing remarks are not intended primarily to be a criticism of the theory of the "Just War"; they are intended only as a warning. Laws designed to moderate behavior in war may be made, but it is of the essence of war to be an expression of lawlessness. The danger of thinking about war in a "Just War" fashion is that, very gradually, we may come to view war as a kind of international football game. It must be played according to the rules, and if occasionally they are broken, strict penalties must be imposed. But real war is not a game played by rules; only after a war has ended do the "rules" become relevant, and then the victor may indict the loser for "war crimes." Yet, as we have surely learned during the last thirty-five years, both sides in a war commit war crimes, but usually only the losers are brought to trial.

We have digressed rather far from our examination of the wars of ancient Israel, but the digression is relevant. How are the theory and practice of war in ancient Israel to be understood? What is to be learned from them? They serve, I think, as a massive and solemn warning. If war is to be waged at all, it must be done thoroughly. There are no half-measures in war; it is not a game to be played casually. Just because a war may be carried out within the perspectives of religion does not mean that the war will somehow be "nicer" and not quite so horrifying as secular warfare. The theory and practice of war in ancient Israel destroy any illusions we may have about war being "not all that bad," a kind of sport played by gentlemen. The war narratives of the Old Testament are a safer guide to the reality of war than are the various formulations of the "Just War" theory that have emerged in the history of Christianity.

Now none of the foregoing remarks is intended to indicate that the theory and practice of war in ancient Israel may provide a precedent for Christian initiation of or participation in war in the modern world.[15] But they do make this point: that if the use of war is even to be contemplated, it is wise to think realistically of its horror and implications, and in this the Old Testament gives

---

15. This is a topic which will be examined in the concluding chapter.

some guide. War is never less than unmitigated evil and its frequent mention in the Old Testament does not elevate its character. It is, as we have seen in this and the preceding chapter, a form of evil human activity through which God in his sovereignty may work out his purposes of judgment and redemption. But aggressive war was only one of the forms of warfare employed in Old Testament times; we shall also have to examine the nature of defensive warfare. Before tackling that problem, however, there is a further preliminary difficulty. War involves killing, as has been made clear in this chapter. How is this killing to be related to the commandment given to the Israelites: "You shall not kill"? This is the subject of the next chapter.

CHAPTER FIVE

The Prohibition of Murder

You shall not kill.
(Exodus 20:13/Deuteronomy 5:17)

I

One thing in human life is absolutely certain: death is inevitable. But although death is certain, the manner in which each man will die is uncertain. He may hope for a natural death in old age. He may accept an equally natural though less desirable death as a result of sickness and disease. He may dread an accidental death, but can come to accept its possibility within the providence of God. But there is one form of death which is more reprehensible than any other, and that is when a man's death is deliberately brought about at the hands of his fellow men.

Death caused by other men may be of three kinds. First, there is death by execution, or capital punishment. In those societies and in those periods that permit capital punishment, it is undertaken (theoretically, at least) under the authority of law; it follows upon the conviction of a criminal for a capital crime. The two other kinds of death inflicted by man differ radically from the first form. The second form of humanly inflicted death is murder. The third form is to be found in war.

Now on the first impression, war may appear to be more akin to capital punishment than to murder, but that similarity is superficial. It may be argued that war, like capital punishment, is sanctioned by law; normally, however, the legal sanction of war will be internal to the state initiating war and will not be a law binding both parties to the conflict. War, as a human activity which results in the taking of lives by other human beings, is closer in character to murder. If a sane man commits murder, it is to attain some personal profit or advantage. The end desired, within the value system of the murderer, permits the expenditure of human life for its attainment. The criminal nature of the act becomes clearly evident in the personal gain of the murderer at the expense of human life. War, too, is almost always undertaken for advantage or profit, but the criminal nature of the enterprise is not always so clear. In some cases it is very clear; it is perhaps too easy to reflect on Hitler as having been a mass murderer and to assess the advantage he sought to gain in terms of the acquisition of power. It is more difficult to perceive that war is undertaken for profit or advantage and that it makes necessary the expenditure of human lives when it is waged so impersonally by the "State" and when the aims are stated to be, for example, "the preservation of democracy." The implication, however, is clear in both cases; the objective to be attained, though it may be a very lofty one, legitimates the large-scale expenditure of human life. It is only on very rare occasions that war is initiated out of altruism, and even on such occasions the motive is probably mixed. Thus both war and murder are normally examples of *hubris;* men assume to themselves a right that belongs properly to God, that of taking away the gift of life from a fellow human being.[1]

Of all the forms of death inflicted by man upon man, death in war is in a sense the most terrible and lonely. The soldier dying in battle is killed by an enemy who never knew him personally, who has no cause to hurt him personally, and who probably does not even know (or want to know) whether the bullet or bomb he dispatches results in the death of a fellow human being.[2] Or an

1. The statement that war is an act of *hubris* will be modified later in the chapter with reference to Israel. At the present stage in the discussion, these statements are broad generalizations. In actual ethical situations, however, they may need modification. For example, if one powerful man (or state) begins to murder thousands of people, would it be permissible to kill that one man in order to save thousands of other lives? The dilemma lies exactly in the fact that either option involves killing, either by commission (killing the one man), or by omission (permitting thousands to be killed).

2. One of the most sensitive and perceptive books on the nature and horror of modern warfare is by J. Glenn Gray, *The Warriors: Reflections on Men in*

innocent civilian is blown to pieces simply because he lives in a place where tanks engage in battle, or bombers dispose of their ghastly load. So death occurs in war, and on such a scale that there are few mourners; it is in cold statistics that deaths are recorded in history. It has been estimated that twenty-five million soldiers and twenty-four million civilians were killed in World War II;[3] even if every name were recorded in a massive volume, one could not begin to recapture the tragedy represented by every single one of those names.

There are, then, similarities between murder and war, and often it seems that the principal factor distinguishing the two lies more in the scale of killing involved and less in the motive underlying the act of killing. But both involve killing, and killing indicates a lack of reverence for human life—and that in turn brings us to the problem of this chapter. Does not the sixth commandment state as a fundamental principle of religion that human life must be held in reverence? But if that is true, how can the sixth commandment in Deuteronomy 5:17 be related to the laws of war and the injunctions to kill in Deuteronomy 20:10–18? We must turn to the commandment and seek first to understand it in its ancient context, and then take up its broader implications.

II

The sixth commandment is stated very tersely: "you shall not kill."[4] Let us first examine the verb which is used. The verb is

---

Battle (New York: Harper and Row, 1967); on soldiers' attitudes towards death, see pp. 97–130.

3. E. Leiser, *A Pictorial History of Nazi Germany* (Harmondsworth: Penguin Books, 1962), p. 194.

4. For more detailed studies, both of the sixth commandment and of its original context in ancient Israel, the following two works are recommended: A. Phillips, *Ancient Israel's Criminal Law* (Oxford: Blackwell, 1970), pp. 83–109; B. S. Childs, *Exodus: a Commentary* (London: S.C.M. Press, 1974), pp. 419–421. For studies in which the Ten Commandments are related to the modern world, the following books are recommended: K. Hennig, *God's Basic Law: The*

rāṣaḥ, which is just one of several verbs employed in the Hebrew Bible meaning "to kill." The verb itself does not specify the actual *manner* of killing, but the use of the verb elsewhere in Hebrew literature illustrates some of its more important aspects. The verb implies as an object persons;[5] it would not normally be used of killing animals, for example. Furthermore, the verb is normally used in the context of one Hebrew killing another Hebrew. It is not the verb used to describe the killing of foreigners in war, for example; the verbs *hārag* and *qātal* are used in such contexts. Thus the preliminary meaning of the commandment seems to be: "you shall not kill a fellow Hebrew."

The commandment does not actually state "you shall not *murder*"—nevertheless, it amounts to saying that for the following reason. The verb itself can be used to refer to two kinds of killing; in modern terms both *murder* and *manslaughter* (accidental or unpremeditated killing) are possible senses of the verb. But from a legal perspective only one of these two alternatives can be prohibited beforehand, namely murder; the law covers both murder and manslaughter, but the latter cannot be prohibited beforehand since it is by its very nature accidental. The sixth commandment is probably the only one in the Decalogue which can be broken accidentally. Murder, along with most other crimes, involves premeditation and intent, but manslaughter does not. However, since the outcome of manslaughter is the same as that of murder, namely an individual's death, the law made special provision for the accidental breaking of this commandment. Certain "cities of refuge" were to be set aside throughout ancient Israel; if a man accidentally killed a fellow Hebrew, he was to seek asylum in one of those cities.

To summarize the results of our investigation to the present: for practical purposes, the commandment prohibits the murder of a fellow Hebrew in its initial context. It does not prohibit either

---

Ten Commandments for the Man of Today (Philadelphia: Fortress Press, 1969); H. G. G. Herklots, *The Ten Commandments and Modern Man* (London: S.C.M. Press, 1958); R. S. Wallace, *The Ten Commandments: A Study of Ethical Freedom* (Grand Rapids: Eerdmans Publishing Co., 1965).

5. Cf. Targum Onkelos on Exodus 20:13.

war or capital punishment, for both of which there is additional legislation given in Hebrew law. To grasp the further implications of the commandment in its initial context, it is necessary to turn to the Decalogue as a whole.

The Decalogue, in which the prohibition of killing is contained, is a part of the covenant formed between God and his chosen people at Sinai. In this primary context the Decalogue had a slightly different function from that which it assumes in contemporary Christianity. Today we think of the Decalogue as a fundamental part of our Christian ethical system; it points to basic characteristics, both positive and negative, of a Christian style of life. In ancient Israel, however, the Decalogue was the basic criminal law of the state. Today, it is essentially a religious law; the secular state within which we live has its own code of laws. In ancient Israel the state itself was conceived religiously. When the covenant was made at Sinai, God became suzerain or king of the nascent state of Israel and imposed upon his chosen people the Decalogue, which stated in broad outline the responsibilities of the Hebrews to God as citizens of his state, Israel.

Given this context, the initial purpose of the law becomes clear. The covenant was formed between God and his people; in that covenant relationship each individual Hebrew was vassal of his suzerain God and as such, his life was protected by the law of God. The sixth commandment, prohibiting the murder of a fellow Hebrew, granted to each citizen of Israel, the state of which God was king, the full protection of his life.

So far, we have reached a preliminary understanding of the commandment in its initial context. It prohibits murder; it does not prohibit capital punishment or war. Thus there is no inner conflict in the book of Deuteronomy when the same body of law which states "you shall not kill" also promulgates capital punishment and the undertaking of war.

In spite of these initial limitations on the meaning of the commandment, however, it does imply a basic attitude of reverence for human life. Man does not possess in himself the right to take the life of a fellow human being. Murder, when committed by a sane man, is essentially a selfish act; the life of a fellow man is considered to be of less value than the profit or advantage which the murderer seeks to gain by killing. It is this which is the act of *hubris,* taking the life of a man, the right which only God, the Giver of all life, has. The act of murder betrays a fundamental lack of reverence for human life.

But if the principle of reverence for life is implicit in the commandment, how are the provisions for capital punishment and war to be understood? There is an important difference. Capital punishment and war *in ancient Israel* were undertaken at the command of God and were not for man's personal advantage or profit. This distinction, however, does not solve one of the fundamental problems with which we are dealing in this study. It is simply a theological statement that God, the Giver of all life, has certainly the right to withdraw life or to command that it be withdrawn. We will still have to examine, in the next chapter, *why* God permits and commands the use of war in ancient Israel, even if we grant theoretically that he has that right.

One warning is necessary before leaving some of the issues raised in this section of the chapter. The use of war and capital punishment in ancient Israel does not necessarily give religious sanction to their use in the modern world. The context of their ancient use was the theocratic state of Israel, the state whose king was God. Thus it was in a religious state, at the specific (revealed) command of God, that war and capital punishment were utilized. Hence, before even considering the relevance of the Old Testament data in the modern world, one must ask: Is there a *theocracy* in the modern world? Is there a state whose king is God, as was the case in ancient Israel?[6] I think the answer must be No.

III

The fact that the sixth commandment, the prohibition of murder, has continued to play a central role in the ethics of both

---

6. From a theological perspective, one might suggest that the modern state of Israel would be the only state even vaguely qualified to make such a claim; but there is no such claim in the Constitution of the State of Israel.

Judaism and Christianity is important. Historically, as we have seen, the commandment was at first a part of the constitution of the ancient state of Israel. But the demise of that state, and therefore of its constitution, did not result in the demise of the commandment. The first transformation was from the state law of ancient Israel to the moral (and still divine) law of Judaism, where it remains until the present day. From Judaism, in the first century A.D., it was incorporated into Christianity as a part of the Old Testament and given continuing authority in the teaching of Jesus. Underlying this continuity and transformation is the recognition of the fundamental importance of the commandment for the ordering of human social existence. In other words, although *historically* the particular commandment began its life in the criminal law of the state of ancient Israel, that law was simply a formal expression of the fundamental and eternal principle of reverence for human life.

In the criminal law of the Israelite constitution there appears to be a recognition both of the eternal principle and also of the fact that only a crime (e.g., murder) can be prosecuted under law, but that desires, prior to and often resulting in crime, cannot be prosecuted. But an attempt was made to cover even *desires* in the Decalogue *(viz.,* not merely murder, but the thoughts and desires which might culminate in murder); this legislation is contained in the last commandment. The tenth commandment ("You shall not covet") has always been a source of some difficulty in the context of Biblical scholarship; in that it relates to desires and thoughts, it is the only commandment of the ten which does not refer to a specific *act* and which therefore cannot be broken in such a way as would result in prosecution. That is, the internal nature of the crime was such that there would be no evidence of its commission which would be admissible in a court of law.

But this aspect of the tenth commandment is its strength rather than its weakness. Coveting, or the harboring and nourishing of desirous thoughts, may culminate in murder, adultery, theft, and false witness; the latter crimes may indeed be prosecuted, but the real evil lies initially in the desire leading to the crimes, and the evil could be present regardless of whether or not the desire resulted in an act. Thus, although desires could not form a basis of prosecution, they were nevertheless prohibited and condemned, for with respect to principle (in this case, reverence for human life), the desire containing within it the seed of murder was as culpable as the act of murder. Hence, as is affirmed in Jewish tradition, the violation of this last commandment is tantamount to the violation of all ten.[7]

From these observations, it should be clear that the particularity of the sixth commandment in the law of ancient Israel does not undermine its universality. For all men at all times, human life is a divine gift to be held in reverence; it is not something to be exploited in the desire or act of murder for personal advantage or gain. The words of Jesus (Matthew 5:21–22) draw out for Christian tradition not only the continuing relevance of the sixth commandment but also its depths in the light of the tenth commandment. Not only murder but similar acts (less criminal in a legal sense) are condemned, for all of them emerge from the inner mental life of man, wherein all covetous desires are rooted. The prohibition of murdering our fellow human beings, which embodies a basic principle distinguishing human beings from animals,[8] must lie at the basis of human social existence.

But this has brought us full circle to the initial problem. Murder was prohibited in ancient Israel, but war was not, although we have seen that war could only legitimately be undertaken at the specific command of God. Within the community of the New Covenant, the sixth commandment and the principle which it embodies retains its central importance, but that fact does not mean that the dilemma concerning the relationship between murder and war is resolved for the Christian. As a citizen of two kingdoms, the Kingdom of God and the worldly state to which he belongs, the Christian is bound by the law of God, but also in some sense by the laws of the state to which he belongs (Romans 13:1–7). The tension within this dual citizenship and dual responsibility is not an easy one to resolve, but certain

---

7. *Pesqita Rabbati,* cited by S. Goldman, *The Ten Commandments* (Chicago: University of Chicago Press, 1965), p. 187.
    8. This theme is developed by J. Ellul, *Violence: Reflections from a Christian Perspective* (New York: Seabury Press, 1969), pp. 145 ff.

positive affirmations can be made. The sixth commandment, and therefore the fundamental principle which it embodies and which was endorsed in the teaching of Jesus, remains in force. Murder is prohibited. Reverence for human life must be given the highest importance. From this, it might seem to follow that participation in warfare would be automatically prohibited for the Christian, because it involves the act of killing and lack of reverence for human life. In general terms, war is prohibited, but nevertheless a problem remains precisely because war (always evil in itself) may nevertheless be undertaken sometimes in an attempt to eliminate a greater evil (e.g., genocide). While the principle of reverence for human life is clear and unambiguous, the application of that principle in a given set of circumstances may nevertheless be complex. Some further aspects of this dilemma will emerge as we turn next to the nature of the state in its relationship to war.

CHAPTER SIX

War and the State

For by wise counsel, thou shalt make thy war.
(Proverbs 24:6)

I

The observer of contemporary events in the Middle East often has the feeling that history is repeating itself; this is particularly true with respect to the modern state of Israel. The Biblical text with which this chapter opens was quoted at the beginning of an article written in 1949; the article was published in *Bamachaneh*, the journal of the Israeli Armed Forces, and was written by General Y. Yadin, who is now better known as a Biblical scholar than as a soldier. In the article General Yadin provided a strategical analysis of the battles fought in the first year of the existence of the modern state of Israel.[1]

The modern state of Israel was established formally on May 15, 1948, but for many months (indeed, years) its continuing existence as a state was a matter of doubt. Though officially recognized by certain nations, the immediate continuation of Israel's existence depended on its willingness and ability for war. It is from some of the early battles that the sense of the repetitiveness of history emerges. One of the early military campaigns described in General Yadin's article took place during the week of October 15–21, 1948; it was given the operational name "Ten Plagues" and was directed against the Egyptian Army. The name of the military operation recalls the plagues which preceded the

1. An English translation of the article appears in B. H. Liddell Hart, *Strategy*, 2nd ed. (New York: Praeger, 1967), pp. 396–414.

Exodus of the Hebrews from Egypt in ancient times; just as the Hebrews of old had to fight for their existence after the Exodus, so too in our own times the Israelis have had to fight to survive.

The purpose of these remarks, however, is not to suggest some theory of the repetitiveness of history; rather, it is to point to an obvious but important truth. Both for ancient Israel and for modern Israel, war was a practical necessity for survival *as a state*. The ancient Hebrews could have stayed in Egypt, where they had suffered in servitude for so long. The modern Israelis could have stayed, perhaps, in the various corners of the world, where for so long many of them had suffered unbearable hardship and persecution. But in both cases, if a state was to be formed, war was inevitable. Theoretically, it might be argued, statehood could have been achieved peacefully, but theory (in matters of international affairs) is often divorced from reality. So the two Israels, ancient and modern, both had to undertake war if they were to come into existence and survive, and, equally inevitably, they had to inflict hardship and death upon others, just as they accepted them for themselves.

These opening remarks have introduced the problem to be examined in this chapter, namely the relationship between the ancient state of Israel and war. Some kind of relationship must exist between any nation and war, for war is a function of the state, not of the individual. That states must form some clear position with respect to war is not only a lesson from history, but something that can be learned easily enough in our modern world. There is still a problem, however, in relation to ancient Israel. The kingdom of Israel, as it is described in the Old Testament, was in many ways a nation state like others of its time, but at one point it was different. Ancient Israel was a religious state whose God was king;[2] the citizens of that state were the chosen people. Given these facts (religious "facts," that is), might not Israel be expected to have a different theory and practice of war from that characteristic of other nations?

---

2. The distinctiveness of Israel emerges not from any principle (*viz.*, there were other theocratic states in the ancient Near East); the distinctiveness rests solely on the person of Israel's God.

Before examining the problem, a brief reminder of the historical relationship between war and the state of Israel will provide a perspective. Then the theoretical and religious issues which are raised by that description can be examined.

II

The very fact that the ancient state of Israel came into existence at all was a result of war, or more precisely, the result of a series of military campaigns. Of necessity, the wars of early Israel were *aggressive* in nature.[3] The Hebrews had no land which they could call their own; the land promised to them by God was already occupied by the Canaanites. Since the possessors of that land, a number of relatively small Canaanite city states, were certainly not going to hand over their land to the alien Hebrews willingly, it was inevitable that war would take place.

In fact, however, the beginning of the Wars of the Lord (see Chapter 4) in early Israel was not to be found in conflict with the Canaanites but with Egypt. Before the Hebrews could establish an independent state for themselves, they first had to win their freedom from Egyptian servitude. The event at the Red Sea, when the Egyptian army was drowned, was celebrated as a great military victory achieved by God (Exodus 15:1-12). It was that event, wherein a new dimension of the nature of God was discovered by the Hebrews,[4] that opened to their understanding the real possibility, if not necessity, of taking possession of the promised land by means of military conquest (Exodus 15:13-18).

The first war, then, was an unplanned war of liberation (the liberation was planned, but God's "military victory" at the Sea could not have been anticipated). If one were to ask whether this

---

3. The debate on the historicity, or otherwise, of the wars of conquest is examined briefly in Chapter 4 (II); if genuine historicity could not be established, nevertheless it is clear that the narratives present wars of conquest as an ideal. See further on this issue K. Hammer, *Christen, Krieg und Frieden* (Olten: Walter Verlag, 1972), pp. 1-8.

4. The new understanding is expressed forcefully by the exclamation "the Lord is a man in battle" (Exodus 15:3).

war of liberation was theoretically necessary, one would be faced with the traditional ethical dilemma, a choice between evils. In Egypt the Hebrews suffered unbearable oppression; to stay there would have meant suffering. To leave Egypt equally invited suffering, but at least it was a suffering beyond which there was a prospect of hope.

Following the Exodus from Egypt, aggressive warfare became virtually a way of life for the Hebrews for several generations. Under the leadership of Moses they encountered enemies to the south and east of the promised land. Under Joshua the Israelite armies crossed the River Jordan and moved to the south, west, and north in their initial military campaign to secure the promised land. After the initial settlement the completion of the possession of the land took a long period of time, and often the wars of aggression were interspersed with wars of defense as the Israelites attempted to hold and consolidate the land which they had begun to control. Under King David the wars of aggression reached their climax and virtually their end. With the capture of Jerusalem and the extension of the borders of David's kingdom to their furthest point, the nation had reached its zenith.

During the remainder of the short history of the "United Kingdom" (under Solomon, David's successor), and then during the history of the two kingdoms, Israel and Judah, it was defensive warfare that became the norm as Israel sought to protect her boundaries from foreign invaders.[5] With changes in the international situation and shifts in the balance of power, the two kingdoms were constantly pressed into war to defend their borders; eventually, Israel succumbed to the military might of Assyria (722/1 B.C.) and later Judah was conquered by the superior military power of Babylon (587/6 B.C.). Though both nations eventually ceased to exist as independent political states, the fact

---

5. There were exceptions, of course; e.g., Omri, though given little space in the Biblical narrative, seems to have had considerable success in expanding the boundaries of the northern kingdom. The Biblical text can be supplemented by the historical data contained in the inscription on the "Moabite Stone"; see J. C. L. Gibson, *Textbook of Syrian Semitic Inscriptions,* Vol. I (Oxford: Clarendon Press, 1971), pp. 75-77.

that they continued for any time at all was simply a result of their willingness to defend themselves in warfare.

In all these military undertakings, it should be stressed, ancient Israel was behaving in a manner essentially common to the ancient Near East as a whole.[6] The existence and survival of states in the ancient world was dependent to a very large extent on military might. The great nations and empires of the Biblical period, Assyria, Babylon, and Egypt, all maintained armies. They were not at war all the time, of course, though war was undertaken frequently. In times of peace, relations between nations were governed by treaties; there were parity treaties between the great powers and suzerainty treaties between great powers and smaller states. But in all treaties the military potential of the parties to the treaty was significant. In parity treaties an approximate balance of military power and influence was presupposed. In suzerainty treaties the ability of the great power to retain the allegiance of the vassal state was contingent more upon the suzerain's military strength than it was upon simple good faith. In summary, when military power was not in actual use in the Near Eastern world, it functioned in the context of the balance of power and as a deterrent; but in all international relations of that time military strength was of paramount importance, and in this matter Israel was like her neighbors.

The reference to treaties introduces another aspect of the relationship between war and the state in ancient Israel. It has been noted by many contemporary Old Testament scholars that the covenant made at Sinai between God and his people was expressed in the form of ancient international suzerainty treaties.[7] The nascent state of Israel was thus, in a sense, a vassal state to a

---

6. For a discussion of religion and war in the ancient Near East, see the Appendix.

7. See further G. E. Mendenhall, "Ancient Oriental and Biblical Law," *Biblical Archaeologist* 17/2 (1954), 26–46; *idem,* "Covenant Forms in Israelite Tradition," *Biblical Archaeologist* 17/3 (1954), 50–76. K. Baltzer, *The Covenant Formulary in Old Testament, Jewish and Early Christian Writings* (Philadelphia: Fortress Press, 1971). M. G. Kline, *Treaty of the Great King* (Grand Rapids: Eerdmans Publishing Co., 1963).

suzerain God. Just as in the international suzerainty treaties the vassal state was required to give its total allegiance to the suzerain power, so also the state of Israel was required to give its total allegiance to God. If Israel (or Judah) as a nation state was to become subject to another nation state, as happened from time to time, then that allegiance to a foreign military power had religious implications. To be a vassal to an earthly state was tantamount to a national breach of the first commandment. Thus it can be seen that the continuing independence of the Hebrew kingdoms was not simply a matter of survival, but it was also a matter of vital religious importance. And military strength and the potential of war were contingent necessities of national survival and independence.

III

It is necessary to turn now to the theoretical and theological issues which are raised by the relationship between war and the state in Old Testament times. The starting point for the discussion is what might be called a "fact of faith," namely that the form which the Kingdom of God assumed in Old Testament times was that of a *nation state,* the state of God's chosen people. To ask *why* the kingdom assumed such a form is to enter an area of mystery (though, nevertheless, the question will be raised tentatively in the next chapter). The theoretical question is thus the following: given the fact that the Kingdom of God assumed the form of a nation state, is any relationship between the state and war conceivable, other than that described in the earlier part of this chapter?

Two theoretical alternatives to the dilemma were suggested some years ago by H. J. Cadbury:

> As the way to international peace, only two paths occurred to them [the Hebrews]: a world empire based on conquest, and the intervention of God. Either the mailed fist and pan-Hebraism, or else such a divine miracle as should include within its scope the

taming of martial men and the transformation of the lion and the adder—these two seemed the only sure curatives for war.[8]

Though the details of Cadbury's reconstruction of Hebrew thought are debatable, the two alternatives seem to be clear. The latter alternative, that of the "divine miracle," does appear in the Old Testament writings, though it appears not as a present reality but as a distant vision in the prophetic writings, evoked, it seems, by the eventual disasters in which the first alternative culminated. The first alternative, conquest and war, was not a distant vision but a present reality. Was it a necessary reality? The answer would seem to be in the affirmative and the reason is to be found, in part, in the nature of "salvation history"; the normative form of God's participation in human history was through the normal activity of human beings and human institutions. To express it another way, the state of Israel, as an historical phenomenon, was not a miraculous state, but a stated based on normative human social structures.

Thus the ancient state of Israel, though a manifestation of the Kingdom of God, was a human institution; it was the participation of God in the historical experience of that human institution which made it the Kingdom of God. But as a human institution the state was subject to the same limitations that circumscribe all other human institutions. As a nation state in the real world of that time, Israel could not exist without war. Since the view that statehood involves the contingent necessity of war is debatable, however, it must be examined in a little more detail.

Any state is established and maintained solely through *violence;*[9] violence has many manifestations, of which war is only one, but war is perhaps the most significant manifestation of violence with respect to the continuing existence of a state. Once a state has been established, it must have the right of self-defense

8. *National Ideas in the Old Testament* (New York: Scribners, 1920), pp. 66–68.

9. The comments which follow are based in part on the writings of J. Ellul; see particularly his *Political Illusion* (New York: Knopf, 1967) and *Violence: Reflections from a Christian Perspective* (New York: Seabury Press, 1969).

in order to survive, for to deny that right would be to deny the possibility of the continued existence of that state.[10] These initial comments could be affirmed simply as lessons drawn from history, past and current, for all history demonstrates the association between states and violence.[11] But the fact that violence, and hence war, are so intimately related to the existence of the state is not simply an observation from history. As Ellul has observed, violence is not only universal, but it is also "of the order of necessity."[12] Violence, as necessity, is a part of nature (though it is not thereby good) and it forms the general rule for the existence of human societies, and hence of human states.

To say that the state necessarily exists by violence, however, may seem too vague and general; one can move in two directions to clarify the position. First, the state is a structure composed of human beings. As such, the state reflects in a certain sense the nature of man; the violence of the state is not an abstract thing, but a particular manifestation of the violence of its component members. Hence, to say that the association between violence and the state is of the order of necessity is in the last resort to make an affirmation concerning the nature of man. Second, however, there is an international (or inter-state) context in which the association between the state and war must be understood, for war is a manifestation of violence *between* states. One cannot consider the problem of war with respect to the nature and activity of a single state, but only in terms of the relationship between states.[13]

The preceding analysis is hardly a reflection of the optimistic utopianism of nineteenth century liberal thought, yet it seems to reflect clearly enough the evidence of history, the views of certain political philosophers,[14] the Scriptural implications con-

---

10. See further E. Brunner, *The Divine Imperative* (London: Lutterworth Press, 1937), pp. 469–471.

11. Though in political theory and practice the state employs "force," not violence; this artificial distinction creates an apparent difference between, for example, war (*force*) and murder (*violence*), though it is a distinction lost on the victims!

12. J. Ellul, *Violence*, p. 91.

13. See further Kenneth N. Waltz, *Man, the State and War: A Theoretical Analysis* (New York: Columbia University Press, 1959).

14. E.g., Thomas Hobbes' *Leviathan* (1651).

cerning the nature of man and society,[15] and even contemporary trends in the biological sciences.[16] Violence is of the order of necessity; that is to say that it is natural but not necessarily to say that it is in every circumstance inevitable, for liberty lies in the transcending of necessity. But whereas an individual may rise in liberty above necessity, there is little evidence of any state so transcending necessity, in part, no doubt, because of the international context of the necessity of violence. An interesting illustration of this fact emerges from the religion of Mo Tzu in ancient China. Mo Tzu, in many ways similar to the classical prophets of ancient Israel, established a religion based upon a principle of universal love.[17] From this fundamental principle it followed that he was in a theoretical sense a pacifist; he was totally opposed to offensive warfare. And yet, ironically, it is recorded that on several occasions he went to the aid and defense of small states which were attacked by the great powers. One cannot doubt that as an individual he transcended the necessity of violence and led many others to do the same. But while violence continued in the world as a whole, self-defense (and hence further violence) was inevitable if the practitioners of universal love, and the members of smaller states, were to survive.

None of these comments concerning war and the state is intended to impose a particular political theory upon ancient Israel; there is, in fact, little evidence of self-conscious political theorizing in the literature left for us by the ancient Israelites. But, in expressing a particular understanding of the realities of political existence (and of the necessary implications of statehood), I am suggesting that the existence of the ancient state of Israel *necessarily* involved an association between that state and violence (especially war) at every point in its existence. The question concerning whether certain moral and religious lessons may

15. Genesis 1–11.
16. Cf. Robert Ardrey, *The Social Contract: A Personal Inquiry into the Evolutionary Sources of Order and Disorder* (New York: Atheneum, 1970).
17. See further D. Howard Smith, *Chinese Religions* (London: Weidenfeld and Nicholson, 1968), pp. 60–68; W. T. de Bary *et al.*, eds., *Sources of the Chinese Tradition*, Vol. I (New York: Columbia University Press, 1964), pp. 34–47.

be drawn from this reality is delayed until the following chapter. For the moment, the fact that the existence of the state involves violence is sufficient. In Chapter 3 I argued that God participated in the history of ancient Israel primarily through the normal forms and structures of human activity. The state is a form of human organization through which God worked in the times of ancient Israel, and war was a form of human activity inseparably linked to the existence of the state.

IV

Having said all this, however, there is still one further dimension to the subject which must be mentioned; it is stated in the Old Testament, but its meaning borders on mystery. It is that the events associated with the foundation and continuation of the state of Israel are worked out within the providence of God. This truth can be clarified only a little in the human language of the Biblical narrative, as one example will attempt to demonstrate. It was stated earlier in this chapter that war was inevitable if Israel was to take possession of the promised land for the simple reason that the promised land was already occupied. But within the providence of God the unavoidability of those initial aggressive wars was justified in the sense that they functioned not only to fulfill the divine promise of the gift of a land, but also to execute the divine judgment on the inhabitants of the land, who are said to have been sinful beyond redemption. It is a point which is simply stated within the revelation of God; it could not be established historically, for example, that the Canaanites were necessarily more morally corrupt than the Assyrians or some other people, and therefore fully deserving of their lot. But God is presented here as employing the (politically unavoidable) wars of the Hebrew conquest as a means of divine judgment on evil nations, just as later he was to employ the victorious warfare of foreign nations in the execution of his judgment upon his own chosen people. It is this latter point which introduces the topic of the next chapter.

CHAPTER SEVEN
The Meaning of Defeat in War

*The Lord will cause you to be defeated before your
enemies; you shall go out one way against them,
and flee seven ways before them. . . .*

(Deuteronomy 28:25)

I

On August 17, 1942, a disastrous raid was launched against the
French coast in the vicinity of Dieppe. It was led by Admiral
Mountbatten, who had under his command some three thousand
Canadian forces and a small number of British commandos. Approximately eighteen hundred of the Canadian troops were either
killed or taken prisoner; by any standards the raid was a terrible
failure.

Sir Charles Wilson (Lord Moran) recorded in his diaries that
he was with Winston Churchill in Cairo at the time of the Dieppe
disaster; as Churchill's personal physician, Wilson was able to
observe the great man in a number of distressing situations. In
the matter of Dieppe, he recalls, Churchill refused to hear the
word "failure" used; even from defeat, Churchill affirmed, there
were lessons to be learned. And later, as it happened, the defeat at
Dieppe was to provide important lessons for the ultimate invasion
of occupied France.[1]

Defeat in war may always provide an opportunity for learn-
ing, but the kind of lesson to be learned will vary according to the
severity of the defeat. At Dieppe the defeat was limited, for the

1. See *Churchill: Taken from the Diaries of Lord Moran: the Struggle for
Survival, 1940–1965* (Boston: Houghton Mifflin Company, 1966), p. 73.

raid was simply one operation in a larger conflict. Defeat contributed to a more cautious understanding of the conduct of war. But
if defeat in war is complete and final, it is no time to think of
improving strategy: a more profound and important lesson has to
be learned.

For the ancient state of Israel, which had been established
initially on the field of battle, the end too was to come in war.
And the end, when it finally came, was so complete that a totally
new understanding of God and of human existence had to be
learned; it was a lesson which was to have extraordinary influence
in subsequent history. But before examining that lesson, it is
necessary to look briefly at the historical facts relating to the
military defeat of God's chosen people.

II

Following the death of King Solomon, the "United Kingdom" of
ancient Israel divided into two smaller states, Israel lying to the
north and Judah to the south. Although the two states retained
certain ties and affinities, at least one implication of the division
of the original united monarchy was a weakening of military
strength. There were now two relatively small states, each vul-
nerable to the great powers of that time, Assyria (and later Babylon) to the northeast and Egypt to the south.

The short history of the northern kingdom extended over
some two centuries; it was terminated eventually when the Assyrian military power began to expand southwards. When the capital city of Samaria was defeated and captured in 722/1 B.C.,
there came a complete and final end to one stream of the Hebrew
tradition. The state of Judah, further to the south, survived for
little more than a century longer, until it too was at last defeated
in war. By the year 586 B.C., the Babylonian army, which had
assumed power over the Assyrians, finally completed the conquest of Judah and its capital city, Jerusalem.[2]

2. Only the most general historical information is provided here; for
detailed accounts of the history and fates of the kingdoms of Israel and Judah,

When defeat came to the smaller southern kingdom of Judah, it was in every sense total defeat. The country had been conquered; Jerusalem had not only been captured, but its strong walls of defense were leveled to the ground and much of the city was destroyed by fire. The king, Zedekiah, saw his sons executed; then he was blinded by his captors and taken to Babylon in captivity where he later died. Many of the most important citizens of Judah holding religious, military, and administrative offices were executed, while the majority of those who were spared were deported into exile in Babylon. The chosen people and the possession of the promised land, so it must have seemed at the time, had come to a final end. In a defeat so total the lessons to be learned were inevitably profound—for some of the Jews, at least.

One of the tragic features of the military defeat of the chosen people lies in the fact that the defeat was a reversal of their own conquest. Centuries earlier, the Israelites had captured their promised land with the aid of divine intervention in history. Within the providence of God one purpose of that conquest had been the execution of God's judgment on the Canaanites, the inhabitants of the land, because of their evil deeds. And now that the Hebrews, like their predecessors, had also lost possession of the land, there was a way of understanding military defeat ready at hand. The Canaanites had been expelled for their evil; perhaps, too, the Israelites had forfeited their land because of evil deeds. It was becoming evident that God was no respecter of persons, and though the providence of God might not always be fully understood, a certain justice was becoming clear in his dealings with men.

However, the implication that the Israelites forfeited the land because of their evil raised an even more radical question. Did military defeat in war and the loss of the promised land mean that the covenant between God and his people had been irreparably broken? In a strictly legal sense, the answer would appear to

---

the following works are recommended: J. Bright, *A History of Israel* (London: S.C.M. Press, 1960); M. Noth, *The History of Israel* (London: A. & C. Black, 1960).

have been Yes; the Israelites had failed in their covenantal com-
mitments, and God was freed from obligation. But it was just at
this point that a deeper understanding of the nature of God was
beginning to emerge. The men who were beginning to perceive
more fully the nature of God were the prophets of the time, and
to them we must turn in order to discover some of the lessons of
defeat in war.

III

The prophets, who were the spokesmen of God to the chosen
people, perceived more clearly than their fellow citizens the close
interrelationship between matters of religion and affairs of state.
They understood that war and the threat of war were more than
fate, more than an accidental result of changes in international
power; in the eyes of the prophets military danger on the country's border was intimately related to the religious and moral
condition of the nation. Hence, long before the end came for the
state of Judah, it had been anticipated by the prophets. They
understood that the land was God's gift in the covenant and that
the social and moral decline in the nation were a manifestation of
the chosen people's failure to maintain their covenant obligations.
The coming judgment which they declared was not so much a
result of special foreknowledge as it was a perception of the
inevitability of the outcome of Judah's moral and spiritual decline. But that perception was in itself a result of the prophets'
intimate knowledge of God; aware of his holiness and justice and
serving as his spokesmen, they knew that the sin, hypocrisy,
syncretism, and immorality of their people must inevitably result
in a breach of the covenant relationship.

　　And yet the intimacy of the relationship between the
prophets and God provided them with still further insight. From
one perspective the relationship between God and his people was
one of law; in legal terms the chosen people had forfeited the
privilege of divine blessings by their crimes. But the prophets
knew too that the roots of the covenant lay deeper than in law

alone; at the deepest level the first move towards the covenant relationship had been made by God and it had been made in love. As a result of this insight the prophets foresaw the end of the covenant in its traditional form, namely the end of the nation state of God's chosen people, but they could not accept that as a final end. And since what seemed to be the final end came in a disastrous military defeat, it was out of the darkness of defeat that the vision of a new future arose.

The vision of a distant but different future was expressed in a number of ways, and for some of the prophets it was no more than a vague hope. For Jeremiah, who lived through the critical years of the end of the state of Judah, the vision took on a more distinctive form. Seeing in his own time the end of the old covenant in its traditional form, he spoke of a new covenant (Jeremiah 31:31–34). Whereas the old covenant had an external form in the nation state, the new covenant would be marked by an inner work of God in man's heart. What Jeremiah had come to see was the true nature of mankind; the failure of the chosen people to fulfill their high calling pointed to a deeper need in man which could only be met by a work of God in man's heart.

But one of the prophets expressed the vision of the future with particularly striking language, in which the conceptions of peace and war were poignantly mixed. That prophet was Zechariah, a man who lived several generations after the defeat of Judah and who was able to reflect maturely on the meaning of defeat from the perspective of distance in time. He declared to his audience: "Lo, your King comes!" (Zechariah 9:9); the word "king" in the ancient world conjured up the image of a monarch and military might. Zechariah pursued the military image: "His dominion shall be from sea to sea, and from the river to the ends of the earth" (9:10). And yet the prophet was talking about a different kind of king, one whose coming would be marked by humility and whose message would be of peace. He would come to Jerusalem riding upon an ass. Were he a great military king, a chariot pulled by fine horses would have been more appropriate, for to ride into the capital city on an ass would have been an almost comical sign of humility. To convert the image into contemporary language, it would be like a President in modern times riding in state into his capital city not in a Cadillac or Rolls Royce but in a ten-year-old Volkswagen. It was to be some centuries after the time of Zechariah that Matthew, the writer of the first Gospel, was to recognize in the person of Jesus the fulfillment of this ancient prophecy (Matthew 21:5).

IV

We must now turn to the larger lessons to be learned from Israel's defeat in war. A starting point is provided by the expression "new covenant" which was employed by Jeremiah. Our Christian Bible is divided into two principal parts, the Old Testament and the New Testament, but the word "testament" is somewhat misleading; a more precise translation would be "covenant" and the word is also more appropriate with respect to the content of the book. The Old Testament tells the story of the old covenant, anticipated by the patriarchs and established at Mount Sinai; the New Testament recounts the advent of the new covenant in the person of Jesus Christ. The contrast can be taken further. In the Old Testament the Kingdom of God takes the form of a nation state; the formation, existence, and demise of that state are described in its pages. In the New Testament the Kingdom of God is presented as a central theme in the teaching of Jesus; according to Jesus the Kingdom was not to be a nation state, but a realm within men's hearts. The Kingdom would know no physical limits and have no geographical boundaries, but it would extend to wherever the King was acknowledged in men's hearts and lives.

From an historical perspective it was defeat in war which terminated the outward form of the old covenant, the nation state; and it was defeat in war which prompted man to ponder the covenant and to seek a solution to the problem of man's nature and the manner of God's dealings with man. From the perspective of the modern reader, however, it seems that the old covenant was a failure, and one is tempted to ask why the Kingdom of

God first assumed the form of a nation state. It was indeed a failure, though the fault lay with man and not with God. The reason for the form manifest in the old covenant may ultimately be a mystery, a part of the providence of God; nevertheless, there are lessons which members of the new covenant may learn from the old covenant.

First, the history of the old covenant, of the nation state of Israel, provides an insight into the nature of political man. Even the Hebrews, with their high and special calling from God, failed in their attempt to maintain a state. The Kingdom of God in the form of a political state was not viable because of the violence, a part of the order of necessity, in the nature of man and of society. The Hebrew people, in their failure, are not portrayed in the Old Testament to be criticized; they simply demonstrate the failure of all men, the fundamental nature of us all. Thus the history of the nation of Israel functions as a parable of warning: political institutions may be essential to the existence of human society, but they cannot be equated with the Kingdom of God.

Second, the political experience of ancient Israel, and hence of all men, functions to bring home to man his true nature, and hence his true need. "From whence come wars?" asked James (though not with specific reference to international conflicts): "come they not hence even of your lusts that war in your members?" (James 4:1). War, in a technical sense, is a function of the state, but war is nevertheless simply a large-scale manifestation of the nature of man. Hence all men need a profound work of God within them, one which will make them citizens of a new kingdom; and like the King of that Kingdom, they should become men characterized by humility, whose message would be one of peace.

V

The tragedy of the history of Christianity is that so frequently the Old Testament lessons drawn from defeat in war have been forgotten. From time to time, in the history of Christianity, the conception of the Kingdom of God has become fused once again with nation state; or the church, as the human organization of the citizens of the Kingdom of God, has taken upon itself the functions of a nation state.[3] For the church, in any of its human forms, to function as a nation state or for any nation state to be identified directly with the Kingdom of God amounts to a failure of the citizens of that Kingdom to have learned the lessons of defeat in war, which are presented so starkly in the Old Testament.

In 1899, Queen Victoria made a memorable and courageous remark to A. J. Balfour: "We are not interested," she said, "in the possibility of defeat." Her words, however, express the very opposite of the message of the Old Testament. Defeat in war opened up new possibilities for the Kingdom of God, which came to fruition in the person of Jesus and in his message concerning the nature of the Kingdom. But it would be better if the citizens of the new covenant could learn the lessons of defeat in war from the pages of the Old Testament, rather than confusing the identity of the New Kingdom and thus being forced to learn those lessons in the field of battle.

In summary, it has been argued in this chapter that the Christian conception of the Kingdom of God cannot be equated with a nation state and that therefore the Kingdom itself cannot conduct war. Whether a secular nation state may conduct war legitimately is a different kind of question, one which falls within the scope of international affairs and international law. But the more immediate problem for the Christian individual will concern his relationship to the secular state. We will return to this question in the concluding chapter, but first there is another important issue to be raised from the Old Testament itself and that is the nature of *peace* in the mind of Old Testament writers.

---

3. For examples of the assumption of statehood by Christian bodies, and the attendant necessity of war, see G. Lewy, *Religion and Revolution* (New York: Oxford University Press, 1974), pp. 71-153, and for theoretical analysis, pp. 237-274.

CHAPTER EIGHT

Peace in the Old Testament

They shall beat their swords into ploughshares,
And their spears into pruning hooks.
Nation shall not lift up sword against nation,
Neither shall they learn war any more.
(Isaiah 2:4/Micah 4:3)

I

Life in the modern world is characterized by certain ironies which point to the roots of the human dilemma. One such irony is to be found in the fact that the two greatest attempts of the present century to bring about world peace emerged in the context of the two World Wars.

The prologue of the Covenant of the League of Nations contains these noble words: "The High Contracting Parties, in order to promote international cooperation and to achieve international peace and security, by the acceptance of obligations not to resort to war... agree to this Covenant of the League of Nations." The origins of this Covenant, however, are to be found in the darkest years of World War I (1914–1918);[1] for all its lofty goals the Covenant was ineffective: less than twenty years after its inauguration the world was again at war. The opening statement of the Charter of the United Nations is no less impressive: "We the peoples of the United Nations determined to save succeeding

---

1. For a fuller account of the origin and nature of both the Covenant of the League of Nations and the Charter of the United Nations (below) see Inis L. Claude, Jr., *Swords into Ploughshares: The Problems and Progress of International Organization*, 3rd ed. (New York: Random House, 1964).

generations from the scourge of war which twice in our lifetime has brought untold sorrow to mankind, and . . . have resolved to combine our efforts to accomplish these aims." And Article 1 of the Charter states: "The purposes of the United Nations are: 1. To maintain international peace and security. . . ." Again, however, the origins of the Charter of the United Nations are to be found in the middle years of World War II; the first signatures were appended to the Charter on June 26, 1945, and the first meeting of the General Assembly was held in January 1946.

It is a reflection of human nature that man's most urgent searching after peace is evoked by the darkest horrors of war. But there is a deeper irony than that related to the origins of the United Nations. At the Moscow conference in October 1943, representatives of the governments of the Soviet Union, China, Great Britain, and the United States issued a statement of resolve to create an international organization, a resolve which was later to be fulfilled in the creation of the United Nations. But in Quebec, Canada, during that same year, Great Britain and the United States agreed to exchange information on nuclear research, and that agreement was to accelerate the development and production of the atomic bomb. In August 1945, only weeks after the first signatures had been added to the Charter of the United Nations in June, the first nuclear weapons were employed against Japan. The "scourge of war," as it is called in the United Nations Charter, was not yet a thing of the past.

Wars emerge from within man, but in wars the desire for peace emerges. However, when the desire for peace finds its expression in human political institutions, the goal of peace is given guarded expression, with the admission that war may still be necessary. The Charter of the United Nations states that in order to achieve its ends, "armed force shall not be used," but it qualifies this prohibition with the words: "save in the common interest" (Prologue to the Charter).

In Biblical times, as in modern times, the clearest expression which the Hebrew writers give of their desire for peace emerges out of the dark context of war and the threat of war. But since their anticipation of peace was not based primarily on human effort or political organizations, the Biblical writers have given us not a Covenant or Charter for peace in the modern sense but rather a vision of peace. Before we turn to this vision, let us examine the general topic of peace in the Old Testament.

II

The Hebrew word which is commonly translated "peace" is *shālôm*, but the word has much broader connotations than simply "peace" in contrast to "war."[2] The basic sense of *shālôm* is "wholeness" or "completeness," and this basic sense will take on specific meaning according to the context in which the word is used. Thus *shālôm* can mean "good health" or even "prosperity" and it can also mean "peace" (in contrast to war), for whereas war is characterized by fragmentation of human life, peace provides the conditions for wholeness of life, both at the individual and at the societal level. Peace in contrast to war, however, is only a limited meaning of Hebrew *shālôm;* such peace provides the environment for wholeness, but it is not necessarily identical with it. And as the prophet Jeremiah pointed out, there are times when men may say "Peace, peace," but in reality "there is no peace" (Jeremiah 6:14), for peace as wholeness involves not only the cessation of war, but also the absence of injustice and falsehood, and the presence of justice and truth.

A full understanding of peace in the Old Testament must be sought primarily by theological rather than historical investigation. The modern historian, certainly, may examine those periods when ancient Israel was at war or at peace with her neighbors; he

2. This chapter has focused on particular aspects of peace in the Old Testament. A good introduction to *peace* (in both Old Testament and New Testament) can be found in the article by W. Foerster and G. von Rad, *eirēnē*, in Vol. 2 of the *Theological Dictionary of the New Testament*, G. Kittel and G. Friedrich, eds. (Grand Rapids: Eerdmans Publishing Co., 1964). A survey of technical Old Testament scholarship on the topic *shālôm* can be found in G. Liedke, ed., *Studien zur Friedensforschung 9: Frieden-Bibel-Kirche* (Ernst Klett Verlag, Stuttgart/Kösel Verlag, München; 1972), pp. 174–186. For a more popular study, see H. H. Schmid, *Frieden ohne Illusionen: Die Bedeutung des Begriffs "schalom" als Grundlage für eine Theologie des Friedens* (Zürich: Theologischer Verlag, 1971).

may examine the Biblical historical data and compare it with historical records of the nations of the ancient Near East. He may trace political, economic, and social causes for the alternating conditions of war and peace between nations in Biblical times. But having completed this task, for all its value, the modern historian has not discovered either the cause or the nature of peace *in the Biblical sense*. The Biblical writers expressed their thoughts about war, peace, and history, as about other matters, from a theological perspective; they perceived (or presupposed, in modern terminology) the participation of the sovereign God in human affairs. Hence the true sense of peace in the Old Testament, even in the limited context of peace as opposed to war, is to be found in a theological context, specifically in an understanding of the nature of God's dealings with mankind.

Thus, in order to perceive the larger meaning of peace, we must first go beyond the more immediate issue of peace in contrast to war. Let us begin by stating in very concise form the essence of the religion of the ancient Hebrews; at the risk of oversimplification, this can be done by using three key words: (a) relationship, (b) alienation, (c) hope.

Relationship is rooted in creation itself; man is created by God and placed in this world in order to enjoy a relationship with God. In the language of Genesis, man in the garden enjoyed that relationship with God before the fall. Man's primary nature, as a creature of God, was that of wholeness or completeness—which is of the essence of peace, with both God and man. But the rebellion of man, represented by the fall, introduced *alienation* between man and God; the primary human condition of wholeness was exchanged for that of fragmentation of life. The wholeness of life, for which man had been created, had been exchanged for a fragmentary life, and in that exchange are to be found the full dimensions of the human dilemma. Complete relationship, with God and fellow man, is the original (or God-given) human condition, the condition for which man was created. To express it differently, peace is the primary human condition, and the memory of it and desire for it lingers within us. But alienation has become the primary characteristic of the human condition and alienation is a fragmentation of human life, rather than a wholeness. And among the many expressions of the fragmentation which has become the norm of human existence, war is but one. Alienation between man and God leads to alienation between man and man, and war is one manifestation of alienation between man and man.

This tension between relationship and alienation continues throughout the pages of the Old Testament. The great covenant forged between God and the Hebrews at Mount Sinai was an expression of relationship. God, in his grace, offered to his chosen people a particular and intimate relationship with him. But there was a conditional element to that relationship, one which was integral to the very nature of the covenant. The covenant, as the expression of a continuing relationship, required the constant commitment and faithfulness of both its parties. God's commitment was without question; constant commitment was also required of the Hebrews, however. If they failed in that commitment, they would experience the curse of God (Deuteronomy 27–28), not so much as a punishment for breaking the covenant law but rather as a natural corollary of departing from the relationship. The covenant was an expression of relationship, but its breach resulted in alienation between man and God. As one reads the history of the Hebrew kingdoms against the background of this covenant relationship, it is an intensely depressing history. Time and again the relationship was broken, until at last, with the fall of Jerusalem and Judah in 586 B.C., it seemed for a while that the relationship had been broken irreparably. In the ancient and continuing struggle, *alienation* appeared to have triumphed over a relationship with God.

But, in those very years when the alienation of the Hebrew people from their God gained ascendancy over relationship, the seeds of *hope* were being sown. The prophets (as we have seen in Chapter 7) perceived the true spiritual state of their people, of which the wars, defeats, and disasters of their times were but outward manifestations. Not only did man need a deep work of God within his heart if he was to be restored to a full and vital relationship with God, but also true peace would be found in God alone, and not in man.

Peace is thus a deceptive condition. Peace, in contrast to war, might not be true peace if injustice and falsehood characterized the nation. But there were times when peace was true peace, not because of the circumstances of international affairs but because of the health of the relationship with God. In the Hebrew theological understanding of history, peace was rooted in God, yet not in an arbitrary fashion; peace depended upon the actions of man in relationship to God. Relationship with God created wholeness among men, and therefore contributed to peace among men. Alienation from God resulted in the fragmentation of human life and therefore contributed to conflict between men. Here, then, the *principles* of peace are to be found, though these principles do not give a solution to every action of God with man. As Job discovered, there remains a mystery to some of the actions of God with man, which transcends the limitations of theological and intellectual understanding.

III

In discussing peace in the Old Testament, it is helpful to distinguish between a *concept* of peace and a *vision* of peace.[3] A concept of peace is immediate and pragmatic; it involves an understanding of the nature of peace and of how it might be achieved, and it can be related to actual situations. A vision of peace, however, has an eschatological character to it. The vision is of a peace lying still in the future; it is the goal of God's work in history, or part of salvation. The vision can be perceived but only imperfectly understood, for it contains within it elements of mystery and transcendence. But unlike the concept of peace, the vision is not primarily practical or pragmatic; its future coming is affirmed, even though all empirical evidence to hand might suggest the contrary. The vision of peace is thus of great theological signifi-

---

3. For the distinction between concept and vision, see John Macquarrie's valuable study, *The Concept of Peace* (New York: Harper and Row, 1973), pp. 11–13.

cance, but of less practical significance to those living in a world beset by war and other forms of conflict.

It was primarily a vision of peace which the prophets proclaimed, employing different words and images to convey their future message. It was not totally impractical; Isaiah, after proclaiming the time when swords would be beaten into ploughshares, issued an invitation: "O house of Jacob, come; let us walk in the light of the Lord" (Isaiah 2:5). But essentially the prophets affirmed hope in a time of hopelessness, rather than a pragmatic program for the actual institution of peace. As G. H. Gilbert expressed it: "The peace of the Golden Age was not thought to spring out of commercial and economic principles, it was not conceived of or desired as the handmaiden of civilization, but it was Yahweh's gift, first to his chosen nation and through them to the world."[4]

There is no similarity, in other words, between the *vision* of the Old Testament prophets and the *concept* of peace integral to the Covenant of the League of Nations or the Charter of the United Nations. And for that very reason the prophetic vision of eschatological peace may seem of little relevance to many people.

The Christian, however, must attempt to understand the eschatological vision of the Old Testament prophets in the light of the Kingdom of God, taught and inaugurated by Jesus Christ. The Kingdom of God was, and is, characterized by both a present and a future reality. In the *present* (in both Jesus' day and our own time), the Kingdom is marked by the work of God, that of restoring mankind to wholeness or completeness; but the future dimension of the Kingdom is eschatological, pointing to a time when the work of God would reach completion. In this tension between present and future, so integral to the Kingdom of God, the concept of peace and the vision of peace are brought together into an intimate relationship. The present work of the Kingdom is to bring to mankind wholeness or completeness, which is the

4. G. H. Gilbert, *The Bible and Universal Peace* (New York: Funk and Wagnalls, 1914), p. 81.

fundamental ingredient of peace. But the present work is undertaken in the context of the eschatological vision, the conviction
that one day the Kingdom will reach its consummation and that
then true peace, the peace of God, will reign. The present work
of the Kingdom is undertaken in the light of the future hope,
and the future hope feeds strength into the present work. In relation to peace, Christians must have a concept of peace, applicable
to the present, undertaken in the light of the future; and they
must have a vision of peace, providing the horizon and the hope
for the application of their concept.

IV

This chapter began with a quotation from Isaiah 2:4: "They shall
beat their swords into ploughshares and their spears into pruning
hooks. . . ." We have seen that these words are representative
primarily of the prophets' vision of peace, but that for the Christian, the vision must be accompanied by a concept; there is
something to do as well as something for which we must wait and
hope. We cannot work out the concept without the vision, and
we cannot honestly hold the vision if we do not try to apply the
concept.

The principle of the concept is contained within the prophetic vision; it is that the instruments of war must be transformed into the instruments of peace, and that the immediate
transformation must be accomplished by those possessing the
weapons ("*They* shall beat *their* swords into ploughshares"). Perhaps we can learn something from our Jewish brethren. *The Jewish
Catalog*[5] is a light-hearted, but valuable, publication with some
similarities to *The Whole Earth Catalogue*. In a chapter entitled,
"How to bring Mashiah" (the Messiah), and therefore peace, the
compilers quote Isaiah 2:4 and then make the following suggestions:

5. *The Jewish Catalog: a do-it-yourself kit.* Compiled and edited by Richard
Siegel, Michael Strassfeld, and Sharon Strassfeld (Philadelphia: Jewish Publica-
tions Society of America, n.d.). The quotation is from p. 250.

THEREFORE: Get together in minyan [*viz.*, a "quorum" (for worship), minimum 10] and travel up to West Point. Take along ten swords and a small forge. Put the small forge in the main entrance, start it glowing, and beat the swords into something like a digging tool. Dig holes for ten trees, and plant the trees in the roadway. Meanwhile, sing "Lo yisah goy" and "Ain't Gonna Study War No More" alternately; if any West Pointers stop to see what's going down, offer them a reworked sword to dig with.

The suggestion is light-hearted and yet also serious, a kind of parable. For if we are to do something towards implementing the concept of peace, we will start in a small way; we will look for means to transform the weapons of war into instruments of peace. As Christians we have a utopian vision, but our concept must not be utopian. Though true, it is no use simply declaring to the world at large, and nobody in particular: "We must all love one another, and then there will be peace." Certainly living and proclaiming the Christian Gospel should contribute to the task of peace, but we must also search for the weapons lying within our sphere of influence and seek to transform them into instruments of peace.

CHAPTER NINE

Some Conclusions

To everything there is a season . . .
A time to love, and a time to hate;
A time of war, and a time of peace.

(Ecclesiastes 3:1, 8)

I

In the foregoing chapters we have examined some of the pieces which together constitute the puzzle of war's predominance in the Old Testament. And now in this last chapter we must attempt to put the pieces of the puzzle together so that a coherent whole may emerge. The whole will not be quite so coherent as we might hope, for not all of the dimensions of the problem of war in the Old Testament have been resolved. But with pieces of the puzzle brought together, it is at least to be hoped that an overall perspective will emerge. The overall perspective will provide, on the one hand, a framework within which to read and understand the Old Testament's war passages. But, on the other hand, it will indicate certain outstanding requirements, the requirements of further study and further action.

In drawing together some of the themes which have been examined in this study, the perspective of the New Testament will constantly be brought to bear. And in the concluding paragraphs some specific statements on the relevance of the New Testament for the subject will be made. But a reminder may be necessary: this short study has had the Old Testament as its primary focus; the New Testament requires a separate and detailed study of its own.[1]

1. A useful starting point is provided by J. H. Yoder, *The Politics of Jesus* (Grand Rapids: Eerdmans Publishing Co., 1972); though I am not entirely in

The structure of the first part of this chapter takes up the structure of Chapter 1; the internal and external issues raised by war in the Old Testament are examined first; then some of the reasons which were suggested for studying this subject are examined in more detail.

II

In the first chapter it was suggested that certain internal problems were raised for the sensitive reader of the Old Testament by the predominance of war-like material. Three dimensions of the problem were specified in detail: the problem of God, the problem of revelation, and the problem of ethics. We shall examine each of these problems in turn in the light of the findings of the previous chapters.

1. The Problem of God
The problem of God was pinpointed in the names and epithets of God: he is "God the Warrior" and the "Lord of Hosts/Armies." The image evoked by expressions such as these is that of a warlike God, not unlike the gods of war known in the pantheons of a variety of Near Eastern religions. And this image of God in the Old Testament is a problem precisely because, at first sight, it appears to be so out of harmony with the conception of a *loving* God, both in certain Old Testament passages and in the New Testament texts.

The first point which it is important to stress in this context is the nature of human language when it is applied to God. It is in the nature of language to be limited; specifically, language is limited by both human experience and human understanding. God is transcendent; in his fullness, he exceeds the limitations of human language and human understanding. But if God were transcendent *only,* it would be impossible to speak of *him*[2] at all,

---

agreement with Yoder's position, his study is an excellent guide to the depths and complexities of the topic.

2. By way of example, at a superficial level, to speak of God as "him" is not to point to the *gender* of God; rather it is a reflection of the limitations of human language and understanding.

and, as a consequence, *religion* (the relationship between God and man) would be, for all practical purposes, impossible. God is also immanent; he may be known, but the language with which we articulate the knowledge of God is limited. It may be true language about God, but it is incomplete, for the reality of God is greater than any words which may be used to describe him. And so expressions like "God the Warrior" and "Lord of Hosts/ Armies" we may understand as a part of the divine revelation; it is truly descriptive language about God, *provided that the limitations inherent in language are recognized and remembered.* Too easily in our modern world we forget the implications of the second of the Ten Commandments; it prohibits the construction of images of God. And although few of us are tempted to construct an image of wood or stone, too soon we construct images of words, which can constrict the conception of God as readily as the material image. Thus, when we read of God the Warrior, we are being pointed to truth about God, albeit a limited and less than complete truth. What is that truth? It has several dimensions, but most of them relate to the relationship between God and human history.

The first truth about God to which this language points is that God participates in human history; it is not the only pointer to this truth, but it is an important one. Words such as "warrior" and "armies" point to the realities of human existence and human history; when the words are used of God, they point to his involvement in that existence and history. The words are thus one affirmation among many of the immanence of God. God is a warrior; that is, God participates actively in the human institution of warfare, which has characterized most of the relationships between human societies, to a greater or lesser extent, throughout recorded history.

It is the nature of the divine participation in human warfare which brings out the further dimensions of the truth about God contained in this language. In general terms God has participated in warfare towards the ends of both judgment and redemption. The judgment of God was affirmed in the Hebrew invasion of Palestine: God was judging the evil of the Canaanites. The judgment of God was also affirmed in the defeat of Judah and the fall of Jerusalem: God was judging the evil of his own people. But the act of judgment was intimately tied to the purpose of redemption; sometimes an immediate redemption was in view, but often it was the more distant redemption of all mankind which was affirmed. God's intervention in human history, specifically the history of warfare, in terms of judgment and redemption, points to a larger truth, the truth concerning the providence of God.

If it is true that history is in some sense a reflection of the exercise of human freedom, it is also true, paradoxically, that history is a reflection of the providence of God. And the Old Testament reveals to us the dimensions of the paradox. Warfare is a human institution, evil in nature; it is, tragically, one of the normative expressions of relationship between human states and societies. But God, the Lord of all Being, is also the Lord of history; he has participated in and through that evil human institution for his own ends. And his participation in warfare, it was suggested, pointed not to his *moral being* but to his *will* and *activity*. In order to achieve the ultimate redemption of man, God acts through human beings. He acts *in the world as it is*, for if the prerequisite for divine action were sinless men and sinless societies, God could not act through human beings and human institutions at all.

The central and particular form of divine intervention in human history in Biblical times was the election of Israel to be the Kingdom of God. God chose a people: he called them to form a state. He gave them strength, but he did not endow his people with superhuman faculties. Upon Israel rested an extraordinary responsibility, that of being the Kingdom of God in the midst of the kingdoms of men. That the kingdom failed is not a reflection primarily on ancient Israel; it is a reflection on mankind. But where human initiative had failed in the kingdom of Israel, divine initiative was promised in the coming Kingdom, that of the new covenant (this theme is developed in more detail in section 2, below).

To some extent, then, what has been described as the problem of God has been resolved. The language which identifies God with war is not primarily a problem, but rather it is language which clarifies for us the nature of the divine will and action. But more than that, the identification of God with war contains within it the seeds of hope for modern man. That hope is for the presence and participation of God in our own evil world, a world which might seem by definition to exclude even the possibility of knowing and experiencing God.

2. The Problem of Revelation

A part of the problem of revelation has already been examined in section 1; God revealed himself to his chosen people through warfare. But a further problem remains; granted that much of ancient history is characterized by warfare, why is it that so much of the literature of war has been included in the canonical books of the Old Testament? The problem, in other words, has to do with the Old Testament as a *revealed book,* the contents of which appear to be full to excess with martial material.

In dealing with this problem an initial warning is necessary. In certain matters the Old Testament must be read and understood as a whole if its message is to be understood; this approach is particularly important with respect to the theme of war. The warning concerns the danger implicit, for example, in reading parts of the Old Testament, such as the "conquest narratives," and understanding them without the benefit of the latter part of the story, the "defeat narratives." To a large extent, a procedure such as this has been implicit in those historical events which were recounted briefly in the chapter on "The Old Testament's Legacy of War." Any Christian doctrine of "Crusade," insofar as it is based on the narratives of the conquering "Wars of the Lord," is illegitimate and reflects a failure to understand the message of the Old Testament taken as a whole.

To use an analogy, the Old Testament's treatment of war may be seen as a parable, but the whole parable must be read if the message is to emerge. One cannot possibly understand the parable of the Good Samaritan (Luke 10:30–37) if one read no further than the passing by of the priest and the Levite; the passing by of the Samaritan himself is essential to the story. And one cannot possibly understand the war materials of the Old Testament if only the wars of conquest and the wars of defense are read; the thrust of the message emerges from defeat. But if the material on war in the Old Testament may be read as a kind of parable (rooted in historical reality), what are the lessons which emerge from it? I am going to suggest two significant messages which emerge from this material, understood as a parable.

First, the war literature of the Old Testament may be understood as a parable of human nature and human states: from the literature we see what man and the state are like, for a parable may be a mirror in which we see ourselves and our institutions. Both the persons and the state presented in this parable are of the highest possible order. The human beings concerned have a high calling from God; the state has a God-given constitution. But the parable reveals to us the downward progression of that state, from its lofty beginnings to its ignoble defeat in warfare. Although the story reads at times like a history of perversity, that is not its purpose. Its purpose is to reflect the nature of all mankind and of human states. Human sin will be reflected in human states. The violence inherent in man will be reflected in the violence between states. And, as Jacques Ellul has put it in his laws of violence, "violence begets violence—*nothing else.*"[3] The violence involved in the establishment of the state did not lead to peace: it led to the use of violence in defending the state. And the violence employed in the defense of the state did not result in lasting peace; it resulted in the violence of a greater state, leading to the defeat of Israel. And all this points to the *necessary* nature of any state; to be a state necessarily involves violence, which usually means warfare.

But there is more than this, for the Old Testament also provides a realistic view of warfare; the violence endemic in the state may result in warfare, and warfare by definition involves ruthlessness and killing. And if we read the ruthless laws of war in the Old Testament and express pious shock, we are deceiving ourselves. War is a manifestation of violence to achieve a purpose. We should not need the Old Testament to tell us of its nature and horror, but it is in our nature to prefer ignorance in certain matters. Our novelists and historians and film-makers all too

3. J. Ellul, *Violence* (New York: Seabury Press, 1969), p. 100.

often glorify war; they lack the honesty of some Old Testament writers.

The first thing, then, that is impressed upon us by the parable is the nature of international reality, not merely in ancient times, but in our own day. The nature of man is such that states will be characterized by violence, and war is one manifestation of that violence. But there is also another way of understanding the parable.

The second interpretation of the parable focuses on the theme of the Kingdom of God. God's purpose for the redemption of all mankind was to be realized through the Kingdom, for he is King. The first historical manifestation of the Kingdom was to be seen in the ancient state of Israel. In a certain sense, the kingdom of Israel was a failure, for although it revealed to us the nature of political institutions, it did not directly culminate in the redemption of mankind. But the failure was essential, partly because it demonstrated that redemption was not to be found in the human institution of the state (contrary to some contemporary political philosophies), and partly because it pointed to the need of man for a more direct intervention of God in history.

In a sense, therefore, the kingdom of Israel prepared the way for the Kingdom of God as inaugurated in the person and teaching of Jesus. And at this point we begin to perceive one dimension of the Christian Doctrine of Incarnation. In Old Testament times God participated in human history; he was known as God the Warrior, and as such he was instrumental in the establishment of the first manifestation of the Kingdom of God. In New Testament times God participated in human history in a more direct fashion: God became man in the person of Jesus. God entered directly, though mysteriously, into the arena of human history, and his purpose in so doing was to establish the Kingdom of God in a new manifestation, the manifestation of the new covenant.

But the establishment of the Kingdom of God in the person of Jesus reveals to us a new understanding of violence; the tables are turned. Whereas the old kingdom was established by the *use* of violence, the new Kingdom was established in the *receipt* of violence. God the Warrior becomes the Crucified God, the one who receives in himself the full force of human violence. There is a sense, of course, in which the receipt of violence, namely the suffering and death of Jesus on the cross, is also an act of conquest; it is the conquest of evil, the defeat of principalities and powers. But therein lies the new principle of the Kingdom established by Jesus; its strength lies not in the exercise of violence, but in the humble act of submission to violence. And it is in the light of this fundamental change of principle that the tragedy of so much of Christian history may be seen. Over and over again, Christians have forgotten that God the Warrior became the Crucified God.

Thus the problem of revelation may be partially resolved. In part, the war literature of the Old Testament serves to illustrate for us the reality of the human situation, the violence which is endemic in man and society; that illumination will be important at a later point in this chapter. And in part, the Old Testament prepares us for the New Testament and the transformation of the Kingdom of God which appears in the person of Jesus. And although parts of the problem remain, the Old Testament war literature has this great merit: it is characterized by realism. It does not draw a false and romantic picture of the reality of the human situation, and consequently it forces us to face up to the reality of our own world.

3. The Problem of Ethics

Since war is a problem in our own time, as it was in times past, the Old Testament materials have presented a difficulty with respect to the question of ethics. In what way, if any, can the Old Testament be used as a resource for the formulation of ethics? Are we restricted to the New Testament in this task, or does the Old Testament have something to contribute? Specifically, does the Old Testament provide the data for formulating a Christian view of war?

Before one can formulate an answer to the specific question, there are one or two general principles which must be established. The first general principle rests upon the observation that the two fundamental ethical insights of the Old Testament are re-affirmed and given authority in the teaching of Jesus. When Jesus affirmed that the first and great commandment was to love God with the totality of our being, and that the second was to love our neighbor as ourselves, he was affirming the essence of Judaism, for both the great commandments which he uttered were quoted from the Torah. Thus the principle of love, fundamental in the Old Testament, must remain as a fundamental of Christian ethical thinking.

When one moves from the fundamental principles to the particular laws, there is a more complex situation. The Ten Commandments were, in their original context, the constitution and criminal law of a theocratic state, Israel. They cannot be adopted within Christianity without a process of "translation." Likewise, the detailed, casuistic law of the Books of Moses was initially the body of law belonging to a particular state in a particular geographical location in a particular period of human history. Again, that law cannot be adopted within Christianity without a process of "translation." An illustration might clarify what is meant by "translation" in this context. Imagine that there were a local by-law in a small community in the Canadian North West Territories: "You shall not knock down, destroy, or otherwise damage your neighbor's igloo." Now clearly it would be ridiculous to transfer that law from the North West Territories and incorporate it in the legislation of a city like Miami. Nevertheless, the law contains a principle which is applicable equally in the Arctic and Florida, namely the preservation and protection of homes. In other words, the by-law from the North could easily be translated in such a fashion as to make it applicable in the South. In some cases, this principle of translation can be effected with reference to Old Testament ethical and legal material; in some cases, it cannot.

We perceived that the prohibition of murder, although limited initially to the context of ancient Israel, nevertheless contained within it a principle, the fundamental and eternal principle of reverence for human life. That fundamental principle must remain as an essential part of the foundation for constructing a Christian ethic with respect to war. Reverence for human life prohibits killing for personal gain or purposes.

On the other hand, a good deal of the law of the Old

Testament cannot easily be translated into modern relevance, for an important reason. The laws of war are a case in point (Deuteronomy 20:10–18). The laws of war are an example of laws which specifically concerned the functioning of the state of Israel; Israel was the manifestation of the Kingdom of God in Old Testament times. But the conception of the Kingdom of God in the teaching of Jesus is quite different; the Kingdom is no longer identified with the nation state. It has no boundaries, knows no limits, but exists whenever the Kingship of God in the person of Christ is recognized and acknowledged. The transformation in the concept of the Kingdom means that the laws of war cannot simply be translated to fit the new context. In the new context the recognition of the principle of violence in the relationships between states remains. But the citizens of the Kingdom of God must not be bound by the necessity of violence; they must transcend the order of necessity. The death of Jesus, which is the death of God, demonstrated that the transcending of violence involved becoming the victim of violence. In a sense this may all seem very clear; we must receive violence, not employ it. Yet it is not quite so simple, for the Christian is not only a citizen of the Kingdom of God. He is also a citizen of a particular kingdom; that is to say, he is the citizen also of a particular human state. The human state to which he belongs is bound by the order of necessity, of violence; it is caught in the same dilemma which characterized the existence of the ancient state of Israel, and the Old Testament has made it clear that that is an inevitable dilemma. No state can exist free from the necessity of violence or liberated from the possibility of war. And the dilemma for the Christian will lie in determining how to understand the relationship between his two citizenships. To this point we must return.

III

The second type of difficulty was described as being external in nature. The large quantity of material about war and God in relation to war in the Old Testament may provide the basis from which a critique might be launched against Christian faith and Christian Scripture. And furthermore, the relationship between Christianity and war during the centuries of Christian history may also provide a basis for critique; although this is slightly beyond the specific perspectives of our study, it falls within our general perspective precisely because the Old Testament has often been influential in the theory and practice of Christian involvement in war.

Let us examine the latter part of the problem first. I must begin by saying that I know of no real answer to it other than admission and repentance. But it is a real problem. Of all the arguments that may be launched against the faith, the argument from Christian history is one of the most powerful. It is simply a fact that a large number of appalling acts of violence have been perpetrated in the name of Christian faith. And it is also a fact that the Old Testament has sometimes been influential in the commission of those acts; in my judgment, that influence has been the result of a misunderstanding of the message of the Old Testament, but the fact remains. The critic may rightly observe that the New Testament provides a standard of judgment: a man is known by his deeds ("fruits"). And a good deal of Christian history stands in judgment over us. It is no use saying that all the things which were bad in the past were done by persons who were not true Christians; God will be the judge of that. Our history is our legacy, and we accept it, willingly or unwillingly, the good and the bad alike. I can admit that. I can, in a sense, repent on behalf of my tradition. But I cannot change the reality of history.

The more serious problem is the defense of Scripture itself. I have nothing new to say here; if we have grappled with the problem, if we have formulated some solutions (perhaps similar to those summarized in section II above), then we have the beginnings of an argument in explanation of and defense of the Old Testament Scriptures. If there is any merit at all in the arguments which have been developed in this book, then our role is more to explain than to defend the warlike material of the Old Testament. We need to explain its theological richness, its implications for our understanding of God, and its relevance to Christian living.

But all this brings us back to a more fundamental issue. In this day and age, the battles in the arena of *apologia* are not central in the minds of men. For most people who are not within the Christian family, the problem of war in the Old Testament will be a problem which rarely, if ever, bothers them. Educating those who are within the family becomes a more urgent and immediate problem. And if Elbert Russell is right (see Chapter 1), if orthodox Christians really are prone to militarism, really are influenced towards this by the Old Testament, then Christian education with respect to the content and meaning of the literature of war in the Bible becomes an urgent priority.

IV

There were three additional reasons stated in Chapter I for studying the problem of war which have not yet received detailed attention. (1) War is a man-made phenomenon and is therefore influenced by human *attitudes* towards it. (2) The Old Testament is a part of the Christian education curriculum and can therefore be influential in the formation of Christian attitudes; therefore, the area of Christian education is vital. (3) We live in a century of war which has become the era of destructive human omnipotence; we cannot live responsibly in this century without attempting to understand the problem of war and without seeking our own role in society with respect to this issue. Of these three reasons, the second will now be the focus of our attention, namely Christian education with respect to warfare in the Old Testament. As this theme is developed, its relevance to the first and third reasons stated above should also become clear.

In many major Christian denominations Christian education is devoted almost entirely to young people and very little attention is given to adult education. I have no particular competence in the field of children's education, so I will confine myself to some general remarks. The first is this: it appears to me that for many centuries the Christian community has been extremely anxious about the sexual education and knowledge of young people, and not particularly worried about their education with respect to violence and war. The Song of Solomon has been taboo; the Old Testament war narratives are adventure stories that catch and hold children's attention. I am not suggesting a reversal in this set of priorities; I am suggesting that it lacks balance, and for the peace and health of society as a whole we need to give more attention to questions of conflict and violence in the Christian education curriculum. I would suggest as a guide that we be very cautious about including war literature in the curriculum for younger children. But it must not be ignored, for violence is a dimension of life which comes to children through different media—books, comics, television, and films. And so gradually the Old Testament perspective on violence and war must be introduced, but it must be introduced within the perspective of the "meaning of defeat" and the "vision of peace."

But to talk of the education of children in these matters presupposes that there are adults qualified to teach them. And while many adults are thoroughly qualified to teach children the fundamentals of the Christian faith, I must add, from my own limited perspective, that I have met too few who have grappled seriously with the problem of violence and war. I have met many who have been puzzled by the Old Testament treatment of war and who, as a consequence, have simply omitted large portions of Scripture from their studying and teaching; many have virtually dropped the Old Testament from the Bible and have kept on safe ground, namely the New Testament. To take this course of action is not only a retreat from the problem, but also results in the omission of a vital part of the Biblical message. Thus adults, too, must take the problem of war seriously, must attempt to work towards an understanding of it, so that they may fulfill their responsibility to young people.

In addition to these two difficult areas of Christian education there is a further, perhaps more critical, aspect to the problem; it relates to the curriculum of the theological colleges and seminaries. It is not so much what is done there that worries me, but what is not done. Old Testament studies are often pursued in a conventional fashion; the history of Israel, Hebrew grammar, literary criticism in its variety of forms—these and other matters are pursued in detail. I have no quarrel with that, for such matters form the foundations of Old Testament studies. But rarely is anything built upon the foundation. The theological problems posed by the Old Testament, the relevance of the Old Testament to Christian preaching, these are matters left to the individual's initiative. When I was a theological student, I worried about the "holy war" problem in the Old Testament and sought the advice of a professor for further reading. He recommended one or two commentaries and von Rad's *Der heilige Krieg im alten Israel* ("The Holy War in Ancient Israel"). I went off to study and found a mass of material of linguistic, historical, and cultural interest. But I found nothing which spoke to my problem, the theological anxiety I had about the identification of God with war. One cannot generalize from a single experience, yet I have met a large number of clergy since that time who experienced the same problem in their theological training.

Some shift in emphasis in the teaching of the Old Testament in many theological colleges and seminaries would be helpful, for the leadership role of the clergy in all areas of Christian education should not be overlooked. Academic study of the Old Testament, for its own sake, is a good and legitimate thing; it is undertaken in universities, colleges, and seminaries of many different types. But those who are engaged directly in the preparation of men and women for Christian ministry cannot avoid their responsibility for relating the Old Testament to contemporary life and ministry. And that, in turn, means that they should not avoid the question of war in the Old Testament, the problem it poses, and the issue of its relevance.

The preceding paragraphs have offered no particular educational program; they have simply contained a plea that the problem of war in the Old Testament not be overlooked. But the plea is important for both negative and positive reasons. In negative terms, to ignore the issue brings forth the spectre of the Christian past repeating itself. Attitudes determine actions; in a democratic society the attitudes of the people influence the actions of the state. And, as we have learned, a superficial and partial reading of the Old Testament may result in positive attitudes towards war, which in turn can influence the man-made phenomenon of war. Thus, to ignore the issue can result eventually in an appalling outcome.

But there is a positive side to the plea, which is the reverse of the negative; the positive dimension also relates to attitudes. If the whole message of the Old Testament is perceived, then the full dimensions and results of war may be seen. It is learned that violence leads only to violence, that the truth emerges from defeat in war, that the future contains a vision of peace. And if these are the concepts which go towards the formulation of our attitudes on war, then our action as citizens in democratic societies influences the state and its relationship to war. The influence may be small, but it is nevertheless vital.

But this last point raises an issue which has been avoided up to this point in our study: it is the question of the dual citizenship which the Christian holds. What should be our attitude to the state, which is the body that may conduct war? What should be the relationship between our citizenship in the human state and our citizenship in the Kingdom of God? To respond to this question takes us inevitably into the area of New Testament studies. But it also requires an Old Testament perspective. The New Testament position must now be stated concisely, but the Old Testament perspective will be elaborated in a little more detail.

V

A key passage in the New Testament for examining the Christian's relationship to the state is Romans 13:1–7. From that text it becomes clear that Paul views the state (literally the "authorities" or "powers" [exousiai]) as being ordained of God. The power of the state is exercised ultimately under the sovereignty of God, and though the state may not be inherently good, it may nevertheless function for the good. Therefore, the Christian citizen of the state must submit to its authority and must recognize the right of the state to make demands upon its citizens. The passage does not deal specifically with the question of war, yet it may be seen to have certain implications in this context. Since the state may engage in war, and since the state may call upon the citizens to support that war (whether through actual fighting or through the payment of taxes), the implication of Romans 13 might be interpreted to mean that the Christian must respond positively and involve himself in that conflict (whether directly by enlisting or indirectly in such matters as continuing to pay taxes).

On the other hand, it is clear that the teaching of Jesus involves the rejection of violence and even the requirement that we love our enemies. And the death of Jesus makes it clear that the follower of Jesus may be the victim of violence but not the undertaker of violence. Herein lie the roots of our dilemma.

The fact that we are, of necessity, citizens of a particular state means that we are bound by the actions of that state. The fact that we are citizens of the Kingdom of God imposes upon us the requirements of that Kingdom. But the fundamental principle of the state is violence: it may be manifest in war, but it is also implicit in such institutions as the police force. And the fundamental principles of the Kingdom are love and non-violence. That is the dilemma! Is a resolution possible?

It may be that to raise the possibility of a resolution is to raise the wrong question, but let us pursue it briefly to see where it leads. The question could be approached in this way. Of the two sides of our dilemma one side cannot be changed; we cannot give up the love and non-violence of the Kingdom of God, for that would be to abandon the Gospel. Can the other side be changed? Can the state be altered so radically that violence ceases to be its fundamental principle? My response to that question is: No! But, and it is an important *but*, that does not mean that one should not strive towards the transformation of the state. This may be seen as one of the ways in which Christians attempt to fulfill their responsibilities as the "salt of the earth." But I have said that the fundamental principle of the state cannot be changed, and that is a point which requires clarification.

Violence, and therefore war, are of the order of necessity, as it was argued in Chapter 6. The argument may be made philosophically, but in this study it is a position which has emerged from our examination of the Old Testament. Thus, for the state to exist necessarily involves violence and necessarily involves the possibility of war. Necessity, however, may be transcended, and the essence of Christian freedom may be seen in transcending necessity, in particular the necessity of violence. From this it might be argued that if all the citizens of a particular state transcended the necessity of violence, then a non-violent state might be possible. But war involves conflict *between* states. So, to pursue this ideal argument, either all the citizens of all states would have to transcend violence, or the non-violent state would quickly cease to exist as it was crushed (without resistance) by the neighboring violent state. Then nothing would have changed; the violence characterizing states would continue to exist.

In other words, if one approaches the dilemma in terms of a resolution through the transformation of the state, that resolution is characterized by a kind of Utopian idealism. The goal is not thereby wrong: it is, in a sense, in harmony with the Gospel. But if the Old Testament, not to mention the last two thousand years of world history, means anything at all, it is a goal which will not be achieved through normal means. If anything, we are further from that goal now than was the case in the time of Christ.

Another approach to the dilemma is to develop a theological position with respect to war; as might be expected, under the circumstances, there are two opposing positions (and a variety of mid-way positions). One the one hand, there is Christian pacifism; on the other hand, there are the proponents of the so-called Just War view. To pass comments on either of these positions in the matter of a few lines is to run the risk of caricaturing them; but nevertheless, some comments will be passed, with the awareness that there is a danger in caricature. The pacifist position takes seriously the principles of the Kingdom of God, but its opponents may claim that it lacks a serious view of the state, or lacks Christian realism. The Just War position takes seriously the realities of international political life, but its opponents may say that it has lost the essence and principles of the Kingdom of God. There are, of course, both strengths and weaknesses on both sides. To choose a side is to assume that the tension arising from our dual citizenship may be resolved by giving paramount attention to the principles of one or the other kingdom.

It is possible, however, that the attempt to resolve the dilemma may be misguided. It may be that in this matter, as in others, we are dealing with the elements of paradox, and that we are called upon to maintain two positions at once, aware of the apparent inconsistency, but also aware of an inherent mystery. I do not know (intellectually) how to resolve the paradox of human freedom and divine providence, yet I affirm both within my theological perspective. I do not know how God is three-in-one and one-in-three; that is, for all my examination of the doctrine of the Trinity (intellectually), I still cannot understand it, yet I affirm it constantly. And I do not know how I can be a citizen of the Kingdom of God and a citizen of the nation of Canada, yet I am both and affirm both. But I can begin to understand how each citizenship will influence the other. Thus I cannot be a *complete pacifist* in this nation unless I am willing to stop paying all taxes: they go to support, among other things, the police and the armed forces, the instruments of violence. But they are *necessary* (though not thereby *good*) instruments of the state. But equally, I cannot vocalize support for a Just War theory, or for any war my nation may undertake, for violence, though of the order of necessity, is always evil, always contrary to the principles of the Kingdom of God, even if its intention is "good"—e.g., the attempt to prevent genocide.

Now these remarks may seem to have all the hallmarks of a "woolly" position, neither one thing nor the other. In a sense that is true. Nevertheless, I think it may be inevitable. It is, I believe, one of the implications of being *in* the world, but not *of* it. I am an escapist if I think that I can live apart from society, apart from belonging to a state. But I am wrong if I think that I can justify the exercise of violence by my state. To live in the world involves belonging to a state; to function responsibly in that state involves, directly or indirectly, participation in violence. I cannot escape that; I must share not only responsibility, but also *guilt*, without attempting to justify it. But for the citizen of the Kingdom of God to be a citizen of this worldly state imposes another responsibility; he must also work towards the transformation of the state. The actual transformation will remain a part of the vision of peace, but the work towards the transformation is a necessary requisite of dual citizenship. We are called to be two citizens at one and the same time, and that means that we must live with tension, an inner tension which will affect many parts of our daily living. It is a far more difficult thing to live with this real paradox of citizenship than it is to acquiesce to an intellectual paradox. And yet that, I believe, is what we are called upon to do. In a sense, we are citizens of the Old Israel and the New Israel at the same time. The Old Israel is the reality of political existence in an evil world; the New Israel is the anticipation of the eschatological consummation of the Kingdom of God.

VI

I must end on a note of qualified hope. The Old Testament prophets spoke of a time, distant in the future, when the weapons of war would be transformed into the instruments of peace. They transcended the physical evidence of their own lifetimes, the evidence of human conflict, and aspired to a peace that lay beyond. But there was another Old Testament writer who could not take the leap of faith demonstrated by the prophets. His name was Ecclesiastes, or more properly Qoheleth, and his was a more cynical frame of mind. This chapter opened with some of his words: there is "a time of war, and a time of peace" (Ecclesiastes 3:8). Of all the writers in the Old Testament Qoheleth is perhaps the most realistic. He observed his world with a cold eye, and for all the affirmations from the great religious figures about divine love and justice, he knew that the poor died in their poverty and the oppressed were not released from their oppression.

I am going to suggest that as citizens of a human state, we need something of the worldly realism of Qoheleth. As citizens of the Kingdom of God, we need the soaring hope and vision of the prophets. Somehow, out of the fusion of those two perspectives, there emerges that tension of belief which enables us to live with our world, to work for our world, and to cling to the hope for the consummation of the Kingdom of God, when war shall be no more.

Suggestions for Further Study

A good starting point for further study of the problem of war in the Old Testament is provided by the late George Ernest Wright's *The Old Testament and Theology* (New York: Harper and Row, 1969); two chapters in this book, "God the Lord" and "God the Warrior," are particularly pertinent to the subject. One might not agree with every point made by Wright, but he is one of the few Old Testament scholars to have taken the subject seriously in a theological context. A shorter study by Patrick D. Miller, Jr., will also be found very helpful: "God the Warrior: A Problem in Biblical Interpretation and Apologetics," *Interpretation* 19 (1965), 39–46.

Waldemar Janzen, a Mennonite scholar representing the pacifist tradition within Christianity, has written a very fine article in the Wright memorial volume: "God as Warrior and Lord: A Conversation with G. E. Wright," *Bulletin of the American Schools of Oriental Research* 220 (1975), 73–75. With sympathy and insight he offers a different perspective on the same data which was employed by Wright. Janzen has also written a very useful survey article on the same subject: "War in the Old Testament," *Mennonite Quarterly Review* 46 (1972), 155–166. Jacob J. Enz, also a Mennonite scholar, has written *The Christian and Warfare: The Roots of Pacifism in the Old Testament* (Scottdale: Herald Press, 1972); although this is a book characterized by spirituality and insight, I did not find that it met the expectations evoked by the title.

In order to gain a wider perspective on the subject, one must move from the Old Testament into the New Testament period and the history of Christianity. For the New Testament, John Howard Yoder's *The Politics of Jesus* (Grand Rapids: Eerdmans

113

Publishing Co., 1972) will provide an excellent starting point from a pacifist point of view. For a broader picture covering the history of Christianity, a classic study which amply repays careful reading is Roland H. Bainton's *Christian Attitudes toward War and Peace: A Historical Survey and Critical Evaluation* (Nashville: Abingdon Press, 1960); Bainton's book treats the subject from ancient times down to the present century.

There are two other works which I would recommend, though they are not related specifically to the Old Testament. The first is by Jacques Ellul: *Violence: Reflections from a Christian Perspective* (New York: Seabury Press, 1969); even if one does not always agree with Ellul, one cannot but be moved by his insight and his rooting in Christian realism. The second is J. Glenn Gray's *The Warriors: Reflections on Men in Battle* (New York: Harper Torchbooks edition, 1967). It is too easy to study war in the abstract, with little or no understanding of what it is; Gray portrays in a profound and human way the nature of modern warfare.

It is clear that the suggestions for further study provided here are few and limited; this is in no sense a comprehensive bibliography. But these books will be a start, and many of them provide a perspective very different from that maintained in this book. For additional, more detailed reading, the many books and articles cited in the footnotes may prove valuable.

Appendix: War and Religion in the Ancient Near East

The wars of ancient Israel were fought in the cultural and historical context of Near Eastern civilizations. It is this cultural and religious environment of Israel's wars which forms the substance of the Appendix.

It must first be stressed, however, that the purpose of this Appendix is in no sense apologetic. It is sometimes argued that Israel's conduct of war was not nearly so bad or ruthless as that of neighboring nations,[1] as though that somehow reduced the problem of war in the Old Testament. From a different perspective it is sometimes argued that Israel's conduct of war was in all essentials the same as that of neighboring nations, and that as a consequence "Yahweh the man of war is only a distant, very blurred image of the God and Father whose character is revealed in Jesus of Nazareth."[2] I do not agree with either of these views, nor do they reflect the intention of the Appendix. Furthermore, it is not intended to trace the historical origins of Israel's theory and practice of war. That is a legitimate task, but it is not undertaken here.

The purpose of the Appendix is simply to provide an understanding of the world in which the wars of Israel were conducted. To fight a war, after all, involves the presence of enemies; Israel's enemies were the great empires and the minor states which together constituted Near Eastern civilization. What were they

1. See, for example, H. Kruse, "Ethos Victoriae in Vetere Testamento," *Verbum Domini* 30 (1952), 8ff. and 79.
2. Peter W. Mackay, *Violence: Right or Wrong?* (Waco, Texas: Word Books, 1973), p. 64.

like? How did they practice war? What was their religious understanding of warfare? The purpose of the Appendix is to provide brief responses to questions such as these.

In practice, however, it would be an enormous task to undertake answering these questions for all the Near Eastern nations. Consequently, our attention in this Appendix will be limited to the theme of war and religion in ancient Mesopotamia (Babylon and Assyria); there are some differences between Mesopotamia, Syria-Palestine, and Egypt, but the Mesopotamian perspective will provide a reasonably balanced view.[3] The survey of the relationship between religion and war in Mesopotamia is not limited chronologically, but I have attempted to give some focus to the Biblical period (13th-6th centuries B.C.).[4]

There are two aspects of the relationship between war and religion which will be examined. The first aspect involves an examination of the historical texts which contain records of military engagements and the attendant religious practices. The second aspect relates to the ideological or theological relationship between war and religion, insofar as it is possible to recover such a relationship from the extant sources. But before taking up either of these two points, it is necessary first to provide a few introductory remarks on the conception of the state in Mesopotamia; it is only against this background that the function of war and its relation to religion can be properly understood.

Whereas in the third millennium B.C. the political structure of Mesopotamia consisted of a number of city states, by the second millennium it was the nation state that was the characteristic political unit. From a religious point of view, however, the nation state was not a primary structure; rather, it was an adjunct to the sovereign state which was the ultimate sovereign

3. For a broader perspective, see Jacques Harmand, *La guerre antique de Sumer à Rome* (Paris: Presses Universitaires de France, 1973), particularly pp. 48–64.

4. For further studies of this topic, see the following: T. Fish, "War and Religion in Ancient Mesopotamia," *Bulletin of the John Rylands Library* 23 (1939), 387–402; W. von Soden, "Die Assyrer und der Krieg," *Iraq* 25 (1963), 131–144; M. Weippert, "Heiliger Krieg in Israel und Assyrien," *Zeitschrift für die alttestamentliche Wissenschaft* 84 (1972), 460–495.

body in Mesopotamia.[5] In the political structure there was first the sovereign or cosmic state ruled by the gods; the chief of the gods was also the principal god of the nation state. After the cosmic state came the nation state ruled by the king. The king received his authority from the chief among the gods and was responsible to him for the proper execution of that authority. The function of the nation state was to serve and benefit the gods, as it had been for the city states in earlier times. But in more specific terms the function of the king within the nation state involved not only the maintenance of internal order but also the preservation of the state against external forces. The conduct of external war, initially on a defensive basis, fell directly within the realm of the religious function of the king.

The historical texts which document particular military engagements reflect quite clearly the religious dimension of war and also indicate the central role of the king in the conduct of war. In order to illustrate the principle in more detail, the particular religious practices which were related to war must now be examined. The following observations are based mainly on Assyrian historical texts, ranging approximately over the period from the rise of Israel as a nation to the fall of the kingdoms.[6] The remarks have thus a certain contemporaneity with the Israelite traditions. In addition, however, the general practices which are to be described are similar to those known in Mesopotamia in earlier times; in instances where the contrary is clearly indicated, the distinction will be noted in the discussion.

The religious features of the conduct of war can be grouped conveniently into three types: first, there are those procedures which were undertaken prior to going to war; second, there are the religious features of the battle itself; third, there were certain religious ceremonies undertaken on the return from battle.

5. For further details, see the essay by T. Jacobsen in H. Frankfort, ed., *Before Philosophy* (Harmondsworth: Penguin Books, 1949).

6. For a collection of Assyrian historical texts in translation, see J. B. Pritchard, ed., *Ancient Near Eastern Texts relating to the Old Testament*, 2nd ed. (Princeton: Princeton University Press, 1955), particularly pp. 269–300. The notes which follow are based upon texts from this volume, and also from the Epic of Tukulti-Ninurta.

Before departing for war, a number of religious activities were pursued which had the principal aim of seeking to determine beforehand the outcome of the battle. The king would consult omens to discover whether the conditions were favorable for battle; the omens would be interpreted for him by *barû*-priests (diviners) or by royal astrologers, their observations often based on phenomena as distinct as astrological movements or the markings on the surface of a sheep's liver. In addition to consulting the omens, the king would endeavor to receive oracles from the gods (principally Ashur, the national god of Assyria, and Ishtar, a goddess who included war among her various activities). The oracles would be delivered to the king by oracular priests or priestesses, but in form the oracle would be expressed as the actual words of the god or goddess. In positive cases the oracle would contain an assurance to the king of strength and victory in the coming conflict. The king might also offer prayers before the battle, requesting help and victory in the coming engagement. Although the content of the prayer varied, in some instances the reason for war was made clear in the request for divine aid. In a prayer of Tukulti-Ninurta,[7] the king called to mind a covenant between his predecessor and the god; the action of Tukulti-Ninurta's enemy was interpreted as a violation of that covenant, and on that basis divine aid was invoked for the coming battle. When these various preliminary activities had been completed, the king and his armies would depart for war. The departure itself was given religious significance, for the king would declare as he left the city that his departure was "at the order of (the god) Ashur."

The religious aspects of the actual fighting are more difficult to describe. Apart from brief references in the historical texts the fuller battle descriptions are poetic in form and may be more indicative of later reflection than they are descriptive of the event. In the poetic sources the gods themselves are described as participating in the fighting and the Assyrian army is referred to as

7. See R. C. Thompson, "The Excavations on the Temple of Nabu at Nineveh," *Archaeologia* 29 (1926), 133 (lines 12–25).

the army of the god Ashur. Though this type of language is poetic and religious, it is not without some basis in fact. That is to say, the presence of the gods in battle was symbolized visually by the standards and flags carried by the armies and also by the presence of priests and diviners who represented the gods physically. In particular, the influence of the *barû*-priests was so great that they accompanied the king into battle and held a great deal of military authority.[8] It is clear, then, that the battle was an affair of religion. It was undertaken only with divine approval, and in such instances the help and presence (in a representative sense) of the gods could be counted on.

After the battle, when victory had been won, military success was attributed to Ashur and other gods who had given aid during the fighting. The Assyrian interpretation of victory follows naturally from the pre-battle practices and the belief in the presence of the gods in the battle. According to the historical texts, the king was in no way diffident about the greatness of his military triumphs, and yet he also expressed his subservience to and dependence on the gods for final victory. The acknowledgment of divine aid was given formal expression in the offering of sacrifices to the gods on the return from battle. In addition to the offering of sacrifices, a monument might be set up to commemorate the victory.

From this brief survey it has become clear that at each step in the conduct of war, there was a distinctly religious dimension. This religious dimension is clarified still further by the attitude of the Assyrians to their enemies. The enemies are criticized for being self-confident and for forgetting the superior might of the Assyrian gods; implicit in this type of criticism may be a reference to a broken treaty, the treaty having been ratified in the first place with the god Ashur as witness. The breaking of the treaty was by implication a snub to the god Ashur, an assertion by the enemy that their gods were equal to Ashur in strength. Thus in military exploits against an enemy who was guilty of having

8. See A. Haldar, *Associations of Cult Prophets Among the Ancient Semites* (Uppsala, 1945), pp. 65–66.

broken a treaty, a major motivating factor was the vindication of the honor of the national god.

Up to this point it has become clear that in practice there was an intimate relationship held to exist between religion and the conduct of war. The problem which must now be examined concerns the ideological or theological basis of this relationship. The beginning of an answer to this problem is provided by an examination of the Mesopotamian cosmological reflections as they appear in the principal creation story. The Babylonian story of creation, *Enuma Elish,* which may be taken as representative of this cosmological reflection,[9] recounts not only the creation of the world, but also the establishment of an ordered cosmic state among the gods. The point of significance in this context is the means by which this ordered cosmos was obtained. It was secured by the action of a champion among the gods, namely, the god Marduk; the champion engaged in battle with the encroaching powers of chaos, represented by the goddess Tiamat, and by his victory Marduk ensured the perpetuity of the ordered cosmic state. In other words, the cosmic state, on which the nation state was patterned, was established by the military exploits and victories of the god Marduk. The principle involved is that the threat to all order is a force of chaos and that chaos must be attacked and defeated if order is to be maintained. At the level of the nation state any threat to the maintenance of order in the state was a threat of impending chaos; as the nation state was within the realm of the god Marduk, the continuance of the ordered structure of the state against the impending threat of an external

---

9. The creation story, in its present form, would seem to date from the Old Babylonian Period (early second millennium B.C.). The extant *text,* however, comes from the Assyrian period and apparently was used in that period with suitable modifications. Although direct evidence is lacking, the origins of the myth probably antedate the Babylonian Dynasty. In summary, the type of reflection represented in the myth is probably not unrepresentative of Mesopotamia as a whole. It should be noted, however, that the conflict motif (which is central to the present interest) may perhaps have been borrowed and adapted by the Mesopotamians from an early Syrian Baal myth; see T. Jacobsen, "The Battle between Marduk and Tiamat," *Journal of the American Oriental Society* 88 (1968), 104–108.

power had to be maintained by military means. Victory was inherent in military exploits of this nature, for the earthly war was based on the pattern of the victorious activities of the heavenly Marduk.

In the Assyrian period a similar ideology existed, but the god Ashur had replaced the god Marduk as national champion. Assyria, however, presents a particular problem in the course of its development, for a new feature appears within the framework of the basic ideology. The new feature is the emergence of a strongly militaristic spirit which was not typical of Mesopotamia as a whole. In the early Assyrian period, before the so-called "Dark Age," this militaristic spirit had not yet appeared, but over the course of Assyrian history it became more and more distinctive. The reasons for the change which took place are not easy to determine. Assyrian religion was not purely indigenous, but was synthetic and incorporated many of the normative features of Babylonian religion, so that in broad outline it was Mesopotamian. However, there seem to be two points at which Assyrian religion showed a distinct emphasis: (a) the national god Ashur held a position of particular preeminence; (b) gods of war were very numerous in the pantheon, and even other well-known gods who were not usually associated with war received distinctly warlike characteristics.

The change to the militaristic spirit seems to begin to take place in the middle of the thirteenth century B.C.; in some instances during this period the traditional reasons for war, namely defense or the enforcement of a treaty, are still in effect, but there are some cases in which no more justification is given than that the war was undertaken in response to the summons of the god Ashur. In the following centuries the ideology of the Ashur-cult became increasingly one of imperialistic expansion undertaken expressly at the command of Ashur. There may well have been underlying economic reasons for the new ideology, but the religious element remains central; the territorial expansion increased the realm of Ashur's authority and from the enlarged realm the taxes and services of the new "citizens" had to be returned to the temple of the god Ashur. It may be that the lack of insularity of the world of Assyria and the growth of power struggles at an international level had as a result the growth of the Assyrian concept of their principal god. There was a change in concept from Ashur as national god to Ashur as world god, and the warlike nature of Ashur was such that the move towards universalism at the religious level had as its counterpart a move towards imperialism at the political level. Whether the political or religious element came first in this ideological development cannot be certain, but it does seem to be clear that a change of this kind was taking place.

From this brief summary of the relationship between war and religion in Mesopotamia, it is clear that the Israelite practice of war had many similarities and some differences from the common Near Eastern practices. But it is also clear that the state of Israel was simply one state among many, and that international relationships in those days, as in the present century, were frequently characterized by war. It is probably a fruitless enterprise to argue whether the conduct of war in Israel was better or worse than that in neighboring countries. What is remarkable about the wars of Israel, in retrospect, is the religious insight with which they were recorded and understood. God was believed to participate in human history; in this belief the Israelites were not unique. But from no other Near Eastern nation did there emerge a vision of peace and an anticipation of the redemption of all mankind as there did from the disastrous defeat of the Hebrew people in war. And for this vision and hope we owe the Hebrews of ancient times a continuing debt and profound gratitude.

Indexes

1. Subject Index

2. Author Index

3. Index of Biblical References

Printed in the United States
106318LV00001B/112/A

9 780802 817426